# Dr. Ray E. Short

is highly regarded for his frank, honest answers to questions concerning sex, marriage, dating, love, and many other topics. He is also the author of *Sex, Dating, and Love: 77 Questions Most Often Asked*.

*Here's what reviewers say about this book:*

"Perhaps the best written and most thoughtful discussion of the issues involved in a dating relationship. The book offers the mature young person an excellent presentation of critical issues."

—*Christianity Today*

"The reader is treated with respect and candor. His discussion of sexuality is open and sensitive. What I see him doing is presenting a strong case for a sensible approach to sexuality and leaving room for the person to make the final decision."

—*Marriage and Family Living*

"This is a well-documented, straightforward, explicit, unemotional treatment of the subject. It should be helpful for those who wonder if they are in fact, really in love. I recommend it highly for young people, and any uncertain adults."

—*Provident Book Finder*

# SEX, LOVE, OR INFATUATION

REVISED AND EXPANDED EDITION

# SEX, LOVE, OR INFATUATION

*How Can I Really Know?*

# RAY E. SHORT

AUGSBURG ■ MINNEAPOLIS

SEX, LOVE, OR INFATUATION
How Can I Really Know?
Revised and Expanded Edition

Cover design: Terry Dugan

Library of Congress Cataloging-in-Publication Data

Short, Ray E.
     Sex, love, or infatuation : how can I really know? / Ray
     E. Short.
   —Rev. and expanded ed.
        p.     cm.
     Includes bibliographical references.
     ISBN 0-8066-2460-4
     1. Love. 2. Sex. 3. Marriage. I. Title.
HQ801.S54      1990
306.7—dc20                                                        90-31178
                                                                      CIP

The paper used in this publication meets the minimum requirements of American National Standard for Information Sciences—Permanence of Paper for Printed Library Materials, ANSI Z329.48-1984.  ∞™

Manufactured in the U.S.A.                                     AF 9-2460

99    98    97    96    95    6    7    8    9    10    11    12    13    14

*To Jeannette and my mother, and
to Glenn, Linda, Ken, Tim, Karen, and Mary,
and to all who have ever wondered:
"Is this the real thing?"*

# Contents

# Preface to the Revised and Expanded Edition

$T$ HE dual purpose of this revision is to update the material in view of new research findings and to add new insights discovered or gathered by the author.

New material has been added throughout the book, especially about divorce, marriage preparation, contraception, the male's responsibility in sexual matters, date rape, masturbation, so-called "safe sex," and sexually transmitted diseases. Included in an appendix is the major portion of the excellent current information on AIDS that was circulated recently by the U.S. Surgeon General's office.

Two valuable new "known facts" about the effects of premarital sex on marriage have been added. Also included is a fourth really great decision that we all must make—what we can do to assure that we have a future.

Explained in detail is the technique discovered by the author whereby large numbers of students decide to change their thinking in the direction of rejecting premarital sex.

The author wishes to thank the hundreds of thousands of readers who have kept this book on Augsburg's bestseller list for twelve years. It is hoped that many have been helped to find better marriages, and to avoid costly mistakes in relationships and sexual behavior, and that this new edition will continue to help others for many years to come.

I am particularly grateful to those who use the book in high school, junior high, and college classes, and in church school, confirmation, and other youth groups. Special thanks are due to my wife of 36 years, Jeannette, for her help with the revised manuscript, and for her continuing loyal support for my speaking and many media activities.

R.E.S.

# Preface to the Original Edition

$T$ HIS innocent-looking little book has a past. Its roots reach back to my own fumbling, bumbling, often bitter attempts to sort out mixed-up romantic emotions in my youth. I later learned that this puzzled plight is shared by almost every other person who tackles the task of choosing a life mate.

And they do not seem to fare much better than I first did. Thousands are divorcing or living in unhappy homes. Many of those involved are sincere persons of intelligence, integrity, and goodwill—doctors, teachers, even ministers. The family itself is under fire. Why must so many face failure?

My resolve to write this book was born in a quaint village near Vienna. But my concern about the love problem harks back a quarter century to a student YMCA–YWCA summer conference in Colorado. P. K. Houdek of Kansas City fame gave us many inspired, sensible, useful hints on how to tell a real love from a false one. His presentation not only helped solve some of my own problems, but it set me on a lifelong search.

Houdek's unpublished analysis is still among the best, and by his kind permission, his study provides much of the framework on which this book is built. I am deeply in his debt—probably more than I know, since years tend to dim the sources of our ideas. So to P. K. Houdek and all those unknown others, I now render my warmest thanks.

If this book has a past, I trust it will also have a future. Not for the royalties it may bring—though authors enjoy getting paid just like anybody else. My hope is that it might give guidance to those who puzzle over the meaning of their own romantic emotions, as well as to those who counsel and care. My years of teaching scores of college classes and of speaking to tens of thousands of high school and university students have demonstrated a clear need. I hope this book will meet it.

*Sex, Love, or Infatuation* is meant not only for those in search of solutions to personal plights. It is designed as well for use as outside reading or as a text in social studies and health classes, in courses of sociology, psychology, sexuality, and counseling. It can be useful as a special unit in mini-courses, church school and youth groups, summer camps and youth rallies or convocations.

Nor is it meant only for the young. It is for teachers, youth ministers, and school counselors. It is for ministers and their spouses, for parents and families, and for advisors to all types of youth groups. Indeed, it is for all persons young or old who seek to sort out their own romantic feelings—or who care enough about the needs of others to want to help them do so.

Where case histories are cited, names have been changed "to protect the innocent"—though some of them are not all that innocent. And the book is written so it can be read by all ages from puberty on up.

Special thanks should go to Jeannette, my beloved wife, and to my family; to my colleagues at the University of Wisconsin-Platteville; and to the countless students in my classes and lectures through the years. All have been my teachers, and I am a grateful student. My thanks as well to Marnie Clark, Rod Bakke, Audrey and LoRee Haakonstad, Nancy Crowell, Lloyd Linden, Mary Russell, Jim Holt, the Stanley Moore family, Rhoda Voth, Cathy Pennekamp, the editors at Augsburg, and all others who rendered help and encouragement.

But for any SHORTcomings or mistakes, I have only myself to thank.

R.E.S.

# ... 1 .......

## Preview: The Problem Is Personal

$N$ ow and then some boastful young friend will brag, "You'll never catch me going bananas over some silly girl (or guy). I won't ever run around in a romantic fog. I'm never going to act like a lovesick puppy dog!"

We grin knowingly to ourselves. "That's what you think" we mutter under our breath. "Just you wait. Some day your time will come!"

And sure enough, it does. Sooner or later that person gets a bad bite from the love bug. He or she goes around in a hazy daze—ignoring friends, neglecting school or work, and bumping into tables in the library. Then none but the most loyal of true friends can resist the evil urge to say, "I told you so."

Just how likely is it that the "It will happen to you, too" forecast will come true? Modern research has come up with some surprising facts.

### Few Will Escape

Researchers have found that few people live out their lives without some romance, whether it be infatuation or real love. Several studies show that the typical American has from seven to ten romances over a lifetime. Sociologist William Kephart found that the average college student had already been infatuated six or seven times and in love once or twice. An average person will have about eight romances before marriage—and one and a half after! Further, almost half of Kephart's 1000 subjects said that at least once they had been infatuated or in love with two people at the same time.[1]

Eight romances, some of them coming in pairs! It seems that the lightning of love may strike not only twice in the same place, but many times over.

You have probably already had some of your expected share of romance. But if you are one of those to whom romance as yet remains a stranger, you need have no fear. The chances seem good that at some time, some place, it will happen to you. And probably many times.

The big question is, when the "love lightning" does strike you, how can you know for sure if it's the "real thing"? Is it the kind of love that can sustain a life partnership? Or is it just a passing fancy? There is no simple formula for figuring out the answer, but scientific studies do give some very good clues. That's what this book is about.

## But, You Will Not Just Know

Suppose you're very young and you think you might be in love. You finally develop the courage to ask your mother about it. "Mom," you say, "when Dad came along, how did you know that he was really your Mr. Wonderful?"—assuming for the moment that he was!

Looking dreamy-eyed, Mom will likely give you her I-know-something-you-don't grin, and say, "Oh, don't worry. When it happens, you'll just know!"

Well, you *won't* just know. Real love is more than a blinding flash of insight, a heart flutter, and a tummy twitch! The soaring divorce rates and high number of unhappy marriages show that people don't "just know" when it's real love.

Remember: Your heart has no brains!

## What Is This Thing Called Love?

The word *love* has been used to describe all kinds of quite different things, from quiet devotion to "lust at first sight." There's sexual love and there's mother love. There's brotherly love and married love. There's religious love and, perhaps most bothersome of all, there's romantic love. The list seems endless.

So how do we sort it all out? First let's take a good close look at the main offender, romantic love.

## Romantic Love: A Lie and a Hoax

Americans have long believed that romantic love is the sole sound basis for marriage. But is it really a firm foundation on which to build a life together? Let's look at just what this term means.

In his article "The Romantic Complex," Paul Popenoe listed some of the "planks" in what he called the Romantic Love Platform:

■ Love is a mysterious visitation, which comes out of nowhere into the here and takes hold of you—just like the measles. [It] is recognized intuitively. . . . If it's the Real Thing, you won't have to be told. You will know without asking. . . .

■ Love . . . is so important that you must give up everything else for it. . . . A man . . . is justified in giving up his wife. . . . A woman is justified in abandoning her home and children. . . . A king is justified in surrendering his throne for it. . . .

■ It may go as unexpectedly as it came, and there is nothing you can do about that, either. It is not, in any way, subject to human control.

■ You are not necessarily limited to one such episode. You can be a two-time loser, or a three-time loser, or a chainstore loser. . . . The intensity of [one's] own subjective sensations is the real measure of Love.

■ [The person in love, like a tiny baby,] wants what he wants when he wants it, and is ready to sacrifice everything for the sake of his whims.

But Popenoe believes such behavior is wholly foreign to the idea of genuine love. He asked: "Now what relation has the Romantic Platform to St. Paul's words in the 13th chapter of [First] Corinthians? None whatever! The one is the antithesis, the negation of the other. And yet each purports to describe Love."[2]

For those who might have flunked church school or catechism, here is part of what Paul wrote in his famous passage on love:

Love is patient, love is kind. It does not envy, it does not boast, it is not proud. It is not rude, it is not self-seeking, it is not easily angered, it keeps no record of wrongs. Love does not delight in evil but rejoices with the truth. It always protects, always trusts, always hopes, always perseveres.[3]

## Some New Definitions

It doesn't take an Einstein to see from Popenoe's planks that romantic love is not for sensible people. It's much too weak to bear for long the full weight of a marriage.

Isn't there something more solid? You can bet there is. It's called real love. But first, some definitions.

*1. Simple infatuation* is often called a "crush" or "puppy love." It commonly strikes those in the early teens or younger. Usually the object of such infatuation is some highly idealized person who is some years older—a teacher, an uncle or aunt, a friend of the family, an actor or actress. Simple infatuations seldom last long. But when you have one, you may be greatly moved with emotion. You'll spend much time in daydreams and wishful fantasies.

It is not likely that these daydreams will ever be fulfilled. What chance is there that the student in junior or even senior high school will ever date, much less mate, the teacher? Soon the fancy fades, and the person returns to reality.

Such tender feelings, no matter how strong, are not enough for marriage.

*2. Romantic infatuation* is what most people mean when they speak of "romantic love." Unfortunately, they often drop "romantic" and just call it "love," which is most confusing. Romantic infatuation is the same as being "in love." It is what is meant when people speak of "falling in love." But alas, that is much like getting into a tippy canoe or hammock. If you're not careful, you'll fall right back out of it.

Romantic infatuation is in fact a strange mix of sex and emotion—not genuine love at all. It will not of itself support a marriage.

Like the simple crush, romantic infatuation leads to idealizing the other person. It too is rooted in deep feelings. The difference is that in romantic infatuation these emotions may be much stronger and last longer. At times they may reach fever pitch. The persons affected are normally a few years older and near the same age. They are likely to have a much stronger sex interest in each other than is the case in puppy love.

*Romantic infatuation is therefore far more dangerous.* The couple's desire for each other seems attainable. And they can more easily kid themselves into thinking they should go ahead and act out their intense feelings and sex urges. They find it easy to believe that they're old enough to know what they're doing. Sadly enough, they often aren't—and don't.

Such a couple may try to justify an early marriage long before their relationship has stood the crucial test of time. And even if they do avoid premature marriage, they may soon drift into a pattern of disapproved sex behavior before they are able to take full responsibility for their actions. Their bodies may have for the moment outgrown their minds and emotions. Hence, romantic infatuation can lead to a great deal of very deep trouble—and not just for the couple. It will affect their families, friends, and all who are close to them.

If you're struck by romantic infatuation, you will likely be just as unrealistic and idealistic as the one who has a crush. The added danger comes if you fail to see that your strong feelings are just not enough to support marriage or a long, intimate, total relationship. Infatuation is "pseudo-love" or false love. It is romantic illusion. And woe be unto you if you mistake it for real love, then go on to act as if it actually were.

Romantic infatuation may develop into love, but it takes time, lots of time. If you give a relationship a lot of time, you can be far more certain that your decision about it is right. That makes the reward well worth waiting for, even if waiting seems painful.

*3. Real love* exists when your strong tender feelings for the other are balanced by reason and deep respect. You care just as much for the other person's welfare and fulfillment as you do for your own. Judgments about the person are quite objective and rational. The two of you have many values and ideas in common. You share similar goals and ideals. In short, you are matched as well as mated.

All these factors will probably be able to support and sustain a happy relationship over a long period of time. To the extent they can, it is real love.

The Greeks said, "Emotion must warm reason, but reason must rule emotion." That's a rule that can go a long way toward helping you handle your romantic experience wisely. If you're infatuated, your emotions will be in charge. In real love, your reason is on the throne, ruling your emotions.

*4. Sex interest* is one more type of involvement that is often mistaken for love. Sex is a deep biological drive that seeks some erotic expression. Usually there is a good deal of mutual sex attraction in each one of the three types of romance defined above. But the way the sex urge is expressed and the place it occupies in the relationship differs greatly with each type.

In addition, it is possible for people to enjoy sex with someone, yet have absolutely no other interest in them except sensual satisfaction. Partly because of our society's double standards, this is especially true for males. Most men can enjoy sex with a woman, yet have no tender feelings whatever for her. If this were not true, most prostitutes and call girls would go out of business fast.

## Sorting through the Confusion

Both kinds of infatuation have one thing in common with real love: strong feelings of attachment to the other

person. This makes it even more confusing to sort out
the differences. Also, these three types of feelings are not
mutually exclusive. They may overlap. The most passionate of romantic infatuations may include a measure
of real love. And a deep love may contain some elements
of infatuation. The differences between them may be more
of degree than of kind. This makes it very hard to decide
whether your feelings are primarily love or infatuation.
All the evidence in this book must therefore be examined
with extreme care.

Almost nothing has been written solely to help typical
persons sort out their different feelings relating to sex,
love, and infatuation. While love is discussed at length,
almost no studies have been done to understand the nature
of infatuation. This is unfortunate, since infatuation can
be downright treacherous. It has caused no end of mischief
and heartache to those who are caught up in its devilish
deception. It is an attractive quicksand that lures its victims to marry, then sucks them down to despair.

"But wait," you may say. "Aren't you coming down a
bit too hard on the idea of 'romantic love'? Isn't it the
stuff that's supposed to make the world go around?" Certainly not. It may make heads spin on occasion, but not
the planet earth.

The popular view that romantic love alone is enough
for marriage is a vicious myth. This false notion must in
fact take the lion's share of the blame for many if not most
divorces and miserable marriages. It woos unsuspecting
men and women into poor marriages like lambs to the
slaughter. How long are we to tolerate this threat to marriage? And what is more important, how can we avoid
it?

I have an impertinent proposal: Down with romantic
love! One thing we can do is to stop spreading the romantic
love lie. If, as Popenoe claims, romantic love can end as

fast as it begins, we should stop leading people to think it will last forever. If it is mostly selfish, let's stop telling people it is not. If it is not the same thing as real love, let's start making that quite clear. It is dishonest to continue such a deception.

Another way we can clear up the confusion is to start saying what we mean. If the term "romantic love" is misleading, why not drop it? If the word "love" in that term leads people to think it means "real love" when in fact it only means "infatuation," it is a cruel hoax. It should be banned from the land.

So in this book the term "romantic love" is avoided wherever possible. In its place the term "romantic infatuation" is used. Let's label this myth "infatuation," which it is, instead of "love," which it is not.

I will put the term "romantic love" in quotes in the few cases where I do have to use it (when quoting another author, for example). By the time you finish the book, I hope you will have formed a firm habit of translating "romantic love" into "infatuation" whenever you come upon it. That will help you remember that real love and romantic infatuation are two quite different things.

## Researchers Risk Ridicule

Is the "love or infatuation" question such a big deal? A lot of people don't seem to think so. While you're sweating out a grim struggle with the question, you may be amazed to find that almost no one else even takes it— or you—seriously. Many otherwise very smart people will just dismiss your problem as either funny, silly, or hopeless.

Scientists have not felt free to make serious studies of love. A lot of people think that this subject is not worthy of such study. They scorn efforts to learn about romance.

Take this example. In 1975 Senator William Proxmire made national headlines when he roundly chided the National Science Foundation for "squandering" federal funds. Why? Because it had made a grant aimed at serious study of "romantic love"—that is, romantic infatuation.

"I object to this," Proxmire said. "I'm against it because I don't want the answer. I believe that 200 million other Americans want to leave some things in life a mystery. And right at the top of things we don't want to know is why a man falls in love with a woman and vice versa. So National Science Foundation—get out of the love racket. Here if anywhere Alexander Pope was right when he observed, 'If ignorance is bliss, 'tis folly to be wise.' "[4]

Ignorance, Senator, is not bliss—it's risk. How can we ever hope to lower the rates of divorce and the misery in bad marriages by staying stupid? Research would well pay off if it helps keep people from making serious errors of mate choice. What price tag does one put on a divorced home or a miserable marriage?

Search Institute in Minneapolis found that almost half of the more than 7000 youth they studied "spent time every day (or quite often) wondering 'whether or not I will find a life partner.' "[5] It follows, then, that every time some new prospect for a romance comes along, you will raise the question once more. *Could this really be it?* you wonder. And that's a very good question. If it is answered wrongly, it can lead to much sorrow, even stark tragedy.

The old saying may be true: "If you marry on the strength of puppy love, you'll end up leading a dog's life"—or in the dog house.

In *His and Hers*, Dianne Kieren said those involved in a romance must face two basic questions: Am I in love? And if I am, what should I do about it?[6] My book is aimed at helping you answer those questions.

## Why Can't You Just Trust Your Heart?

Behind the "when it strikes you, you'll know it" idea is the assumption that your heart will somehow signal you when you've found real love. No one tells you *how* you'll know. They say, "You'll just know." Are they right? Can you depend on your heart?

Most young adults think they're in love right now. If you're of late high school or college age, or indeed any age—chances are better than even that you think you're in love this very minute.

Albert Ellis once asked 500 young women at 19 American colleges if they felt they were in love right at that time. A surprising 72% said they thought in some degree they were. Only 27% said they probably or certainly were not.[7]

But while most of these young adults *thought* they were in love, they were at the same time not sure. About a third of the young women could only guess about their romantic condition. They said only that they *probably* were or were not in love. If we add this group to the 23% who thought they were "pretty much" in love, then well over half were not at all sure. And we may safely assume that at least some of those who reported being in love were in fact only infatuated. That kind of confusion and uncertainty about love still persists.

About 20 years ago William Kephart asked college students, "Do you feel you know what love really is?"[8] The results were:

|                                    | Males | Females |
|------------------------------------|-------|---------|
| I'm sure I know what love is ....... | 25%   | 36%     |
| I think I know what love is ........ | 59    | 54      |
| I don't think I know what love is .. | 12    | 8       |
| I'm sure I don't know what love is   | 4     | 2       |
|                                    | 100%  | 100%    |

Note that more than two out of three were not sure they knew what love was. They only thought they did or did not know.

Other studies have also shown that people don't know the nature of love, even when they're engaged. A study of hundreds of engaged couples who later married showed that a large proportion of the men, and even more of the women, had real doubts about their choice of a mate.[9]

Few love affairs—even the torrid types—lead to the altar. Gilbert V. Hamilton found that the subjects he studied had 6.7 romances each. Only 15% of the affairs led to marriage. And a study of the courtship patterns of 400 college students found that almost three-fourths of their "love affairs" broke up before marriage.[10]

Leonard Benson did a casual study of 75 students over 30 years of age. He found that they had had a total of 653 romances. That's an average of 8.7 affairs per person. Benson notes that in over a third of his sample the most intense romances did not lead to marriage.[11] Cupid is stupid, it seems—or at least unreliable.

Youth are not sure how to distinguish a pseudo-love from the real thing. Kephart's study found that students tended to think of their current romantic involvements as love, but they rated their past affairs as just infatuations.[12] Don't you suppose that many of these past "infatuations" would have been described as "love" if the persons had been asked to rate them while they were in progress?

So what does all this prove? It seems to show that American youth—and probably their parents and grandparents—are very unsure of themselves concerning love. They don't really know what love is.

It seems clear that "romantic love" (romantic infatuation, that is) cannot be trusted. If you can't trust your heart, what can you trust? What are you to do when you find yourself caught up in a romance? Most of us need help to decide whether what we feel is actually love. We need a reasonably accurate, rational way to determine the difference between love and infatuation during the period of the romantic involvement itself. And that's just what this book is all about.

## Age and Maturity Give No Immunity

But isn't romantic infatuation only for the very young? Or for those who haven't grown up emotionally? Not so, it would seem. Even the most mature are not safe from the siren call of romance. Haven't all of us seen middle-aged or older couples with stars in their eyes, acting every bit as foolish as any teenager?

Or the rich old codger who squanders his fortune on some flighty young girl? Such affairs happen just often enough that folk wisdom has long since declared: "There's no fool like an old fool!"

In our society the wedding ceremony is supposed to dry up all other springs of romance. But does it? In the Benson study people reported having an average of one other romance after they were wed. While most marrieds reported no other romances at all, some had as many as five. Luckily, few of these were acted on and they did not disrupt their marriages. But they did occur.[13]

## Even the Matured Get Lured

If you're more grown-up in your emotional life than most other people, you're still not protected from romance. When D. G. Dean set out to test the common assumption that "romantic love is for the emotionally immature," he found that it just isn't so.[14] The real test of emotional maturity then is not whether you "fall in love" (become infatuated). That happens to almost all of us. The true test of maturity is rather what you do about it. Do you react rationally to this romantic condition? Or do you rush rashly into some foolish, perhaps permanent, commitment before the relationship proves to be sound?

## So Expect Romance—and Be Prepared

Romantic experience catches up with all of us, young or old, rich or poor, mature or immature. And with it come perplexity and uncertainty. If romance hasn't reached you yet, just be patient. Your time is coming! And if it has already come to you, it will likely come again—and yet again. The issue, then, is how can you act wisely once you are, as Capellanus put it, "wounded by one of love's arrows."[15]

Be careful. Cupid's arrow may turn out to be cupid's *error!* You need something better than a soft-eyed grin and the old "never mind, dear; when it hits you you'll know it" routine. When you ask an honest question, you deserve an honest answer.

# . . . 2 . . . . . . .

# The Crisis: Problems of Partnership

$Y$ ou must make at least four really big decisions in your life:

- Whom or what shall I serve?
- What shall I do with my life?
- With whom, if anyone, shall I share my life?
- How can I help make sure that I'll have a future at all?

These are urgent questions for each of us. All four choices will likely have to be made at a rather early age. Most people will have made them, in fact, before age 22 or 26. That's a big responsibility, since the consequences may follow you for the rest of your life—or deprive you of it.

Let's take the last one first.

## How Can I Help Make Sure That I'll Have a Future at All?

This book is about choices, and you can't make very many choices if you're dead! So let's look at this big decision first and give it top billing.

Sadly enough, we must face up to the fact that many hazards now threaten the very survival of life on our common home—the planet earth. Not only does the pollution of our air risk our health, but the slow "greenhouse" warming of the earth may even do us in. Or we may lose that all-important ozone layer that shields us from the deadly rays of the sun. In time, the rapid increase in population will pose a threat to food and water supplies. Even now, millions of our species starve to death each year—needlessly.

And there could be instant death for the whole world if but a fraction of our stocks of bombs and other weapons should be used. Firestorms. Radiation. Nuclear winter. Each could kill us within a matter of days or even hours.

None of us, young or old, can afford to ignore these stark facts of modern life. Nor can we assume that some other person or group—Congress, the Pentagon, the White House, the Church, the political activists—will save our skins for us. Each of us must do our part to press for sane solutions for our plight.

And the problem is not just local. These are world problems that demand world solutions. Pollution knows no national bounds. Fishing fleets from Asia deplete the salmon off our coast and are bringing some species of whales to the point of extinction. Acid rain from the U.S. is killing Canada's lakes. The ozone layer that protects us all is being diminished. A nuclear winter would freeze our whole earth. The loss of rain forests in Brazil, the U.S., and elsewhere is depriving all of us of life-giving oxygen.

Yet there are no world rules to keep the selfish interests of some from doing harm to others. There is no cop on the corners of the world to keep the peace and preserve our heritages.

But we need one in the worst way. Narrow, selfish, short-term interests must not be allowed to rob us of our most precious human right—the right to live safely in our beautiful world.

So each of us must do our part to be sure we have a future. Choose your own path and stick with it until we either mold a safer world or go down trying.

My own choice—pursued with vigor for over 40 years now—is to work with others to get world law so that intergroup disputes are settled sanely in courts of law and justice, not with bombs and battlefields. That is, to replace the law of force with the force of law, like civilized human beings should.*

## Whom or What Shall I Serve?

Whether you realize it or not, you will probably adopt some central, core purpose for your life. You will build your whole life around whatever has the most meaning and the greatest importance for you. This will be your life center, your major focus.

How can you find out what your central value is? That's easy. Just write down all the things that are very important to you. Then ask yourself: "What's the very last thing in this world I'd be willing to give up?" Is it friends? Family? Myself? Money? The chance to help other people? Devotion to God?

One thing seems certain. The kind of life you will have will depend on the kind of life center you choose. A life devoted to seeking personal pleasure will be far different

---

*If you'd care to help, contact the World Federalist Association (educational) or the Campaign for U.N. Reform (Political Action), both at 418 7th St. S.E., Washington D.C. 20003, or call 1-800-HATE-WAR. Tell them Ray Short sent you.

from one committed to the service of others. The life of one who sets out to become wealthy will be quite different from one who chooses to become a nurse or pastor.

So your choice of a central life value—whom or what you serve—is crucial. It is not a decision to be made lightly or just drifted into.

## What Shall I Do with My Life?

What will your life work be? That choice is of vital importance, since you will spend so much time at it. In fact, if you sleep the usual 8 hours out of each 24 and work at least 40 hours per week, that means you will spend half of your waking hours every workday doing that job. And you will spend far more time than that working if you choose a job such as farming or home-making.

So just think! If your job does not excite or challenge you, you've sentenced yourself to long years of being bored and unhappy with it. You'll scarcely be able to stick it out until quitting time, when you can dash for the door. Is that any way to have to spend half the time you're awake on every workday of your life?

But if you're smart, you will choose your life work wisely and well. Then that same big block of time will fulfill and even excite you. The late Hornell Hart used to tell his students, "If you choose wisely your vocation, you'll never need a vacation." Perhaps he overstated the case. Yet few will deny that the wise choice of work can make a great difference in the amount of challenge, satisfaction, and joy you will have in life.

## With Whom, if Anyone, Shall I Share My Life?

Some people prefer not to marry, and that is certainly an OK choice. People should not be pressured into mar-

rying if they prefer to stay single. For them, the third
great decision will be *whether* to wed.

Many unmarried young couples are choosing to live
together WBC (Without Benefit of Clergy). But studies
indicate nine and one-half out of every ten Americans do
marry.[1] Hence, the third really great decision for most
people is the choice of a mate. Who is the best person to
team up with for the rest of your life? Just think. That
will be the person with whom you plan to spend most of
your adult years in the most intimate of all relationships.
It is the person with whom you may cocreate your children
and share your life at every level. Choosing a mate is a
decision to challenge your very best judgment. And a
wrong choice can spell tragedy not only for you and your
spouse, but also for your families and friends. It will be
even more tragic if you have children.

Even foreigners have perceived our problem. "America
appears to be the only country in the world where love
is a national problem," observes Raoul de Roussy de Sales.
"The great majority of Americans of both sexes seem to
be in a state of chronic bewilderment" regarding love.[2]

An American folk song sadly laments, "Twenty years
with the wrong woman." Well, *one* year with the wrong
woman—or the wrong man—is far too long! One of the
surest ways to avoid that tragedy is to be very careful in
choosing your life mate in the first place.

One thing seems clear, then. These four choices are
very important life decisions. If we choose poorly on any
one of them, we cut down our chances to claim our share
of self-fulfillment, meaning, and happiness throughout
our lives. And who needs that?

## What Help Can You Expect?

Help with vocational choice abounds. Young Americans
are urged to give a great deal of attention to the choice

of life work. You can also get aid in choosing a life center. There's help from thousands of churches and synagogues, and colleges have departments in philosophy and religion. Yet if you look for help or training in how to choose a life mate, you'll be hard put to find it. What does the typical high school or college offer to help you choose a mate? Little more than a single course or part of a course.

And if there is a course, it may well be taught in home economics. If so, men may avoid it in droves. Many years ago Ross Stagner noted that we send children to school for 10 or 15 years to learn a vocation, yet we teach them absolutely nothing about marriage, which is far more important than any profession.[3] He called this "remarkable stupidity." This is still largely true.

## A Plea for Preparation

All this has led this student of family life to make this bold proposal: No person should try to claim the high privilege of marriage—and I do see it as a high privilege—unless he or she has had either a good course in marriage and family preparation or something equal to it. Such courses do seem to help.

And what if you can't take such a course? You can still get plenty of good guidance. There are now many fine books in this field. Some are listed in the back of this book. Most librarians, counselors, or ministers can place one or more such books in your hands. All you need to do is ask.

## What Is a Successful Marriage?

A marriage must have two qualities if it is to be pronounced a success by the general public. It must be happy and it must be permanent.

In our culture, a husband and wife are expected to get along, to adapt to each other's needs. It is assumed that enough real love is present to bring joy and fulfillment to both of them. In short, the marriage should be happy. If it isn't happy, it's not a success. And if the marriage ends in divorce or if the two separate, we conclude that it has failed.

## The Soiling of the Dream

Almost all of us want to marry. As of now, 95% of us will do so at least once. If the first marriage ends in divorce, about four out of five will turn right around and do it again.[4] And second marriages are no happier than first ones.[5] *We Americans are not turned off from marriage. What we are turned off from is marriage with the wrong person.* The crying need, then, is for help to choose our marriage mates with much, much more care. This book will help you do just that.

But if current trends hold, that gentle wound from Cupid's arrow will become for many a festering, painful thorn in the flesh. What begins as beautiful may become boring. Her Mr. Grand may turn out to be Mr. Bland, and his Miss Lovely has a good chance of becoming Mrs. Lousy.

The result can be predicted. Many who in their wedding vows agreed to swear *by* their commitment soon find that they are swearing *at* it. They become disillusioned, dissatisfied—and divorced. Their marriages move from rapture to rupture.

Your marriage may or may not be made in heaven, as tradition suggests. But one thing is certain. You will have to live it out right here on earth. What starts as marriage bliss tends to get constantly clouded by the routines of day-to-day living. Problems come up with disgusting frequency.

This is to be expected. After all, very few people in this world have no faults. (Your chances of linking up with an angel seem slim!) You can expect problems of adjustment. There will even be some friction. But just how often do such problems change a couple's cozy dream nest into a nightmarish den of conflict? If and when you wed, what are your chances of failure? The higher those odds are, the more careful you will need to be in your choice of your mate.

## Divorce: Our Runaway Rates

U.S. divorce rates are now about 17 *times* as high as they were in 1867![6] The rate doubled between the mid-1960s and the mid-1970s.[7] Unless you learn to beat the current odds, your chances for a good marriage are not rosy. In the mid-1970s, one out of three U.S. first marriages ended in divorce. Now it is about one out of every two![8] Some people marry and divorce several times, a practice which is sometimes called "legal polygamy." If we put all this together, the divorce rate is found to be above 50%. And it's still on the increase.

Census reports show that the trend toward ever higher rates of divorce is worldwide. But the United States has had the highest rate of all. Further, the divorce rate has gone up faster in the United States than in any other country.[9] We are number one—an honor many of us would no doubt be glad to forego.

## Many Hang in There—and Hate It

High as they are, the divorce rates do not tell the whole story of marriage failure in America. Many couples—

about three percent—simply separate. (That's the "poor person's divorce.") Their rift is never entered in the official records. Divorce may be rejected by them for reasons such as convenience, money, religion, or simply neglect. Such marriage failures never get to the courts.

There is another, much larger, block of marriage failures: couples who stay together, but don't like it very much. They stay together because of the children, their religion, money, poor divorce laws, or some other reason. They just grit their teeth and stick it out.

## Your Chances Are Less than 50—50

Now let's put these various pieces of the puzzle together. Just what are the odds that you will have a happy marriage? Take the 50% of U.S. marriages that are now ending in divorce. Add to that the three percent who separate and the 15 to 20% who doggedly stick it out, but are not happy with their choice.[10] The forecast is now clear. If you are typical, when you choose a mate you will have much less than a flip of the coin chance that your union will be happy and for keeps. In fact, it's about a one in three chance. Bad odds in Las Vegas or anywhere else!

## The Teen Marriage Mire

If you marry as a teenager those odds are much worse. Then you take twice the risk that it will end in divorce and failure than if you marry in your 20s or older. Girls who marry before age 18 take even greater risks. They are three times more likely to be divorced than females who marry at ages 22 to 24.[11] One study found that many who marry as teens and do stay married tend to wish they had waited to wed. Almost half of the couples who married in their teens said they would not have married if they had it to do over again.[12] No wonder. Teens who marry not only have less stable marriages, but also less education, less income, and lower status jobs. These patterns last for decades. Alan Booth and John Edwards conclude that "The idea that early marriage has deleterious effects is firmly ensconced in the research literature. No contradictory evidence has been reported. . . ." It has been found ". . . that age at marriage was the best single predictor of divorce."[13]

How can we account for the fact that young marriage is so hazardous in America? There are a number of related factors.

## Why Early Marriages So Often Fail

1. A lot of early marriages are brought on by pregnancy. Such "forced marriages" have a very high risk of failure.[14] Yet half the teenage girls who go to the altar now are already pregnant.[15]

2. The person who is immature in age is likely to be immature in emotions as well. As a result, he or she is more likely to make an unsound mate choice.[16]

3. Parents often object to early marriages—except in some cases where the young woman is pregnant. Then they may give their reluctant consent. Marriages that are entered when the parents are opposed, for whatever reasons, fail far more often than marriages where parents approve.

Parents have been known to go to great lengths to break up the marriages of underage youth. They even resort to legal means at times. If parents would try to help the underage couple instead of trying to interfere, these marriages might turn out better. In some cases the immaturity of the couple seems to be matched by the immaturity of their parents.

4. Early marriage tends to interfere with the plans for continuing the education of the breadwinner. Pregnancy is the chief reason that young women drop out of high school.[17] This may in time saddle the marriage with serious money problems and lead to resentment.

5. One partner may work while the other continues with schooling. In such cases their interests often tend to grow apart. This in turn places added strain on the marriage.[18]

6. Early marriages tend to occur more often among the poor. Thus many of those who wed young have to face severe money problems, in some cases even poverty.

7. Some teenagers hurry into marriage as an escape. They may be fleeing a parental home they feel is too restrictive. This happens more often with females than males. Many families still place harsher restraints on a daughter than on a son because they fear she may bring home a pregnancy.

8. Some women may engage in what has been called "the flight into intimacy." That is, they retreat into marriage because they are afraid to go it alone in a complex, tough world.

I know one girl who was a victim of "smother love." She had been severely dominated by her mother. One night she confided to her fiancé: "Oh, John! I'll be so glad when we get married. Then I won't ever have to make any more decisions!" Needless to say, John ran away from her like a scared jackrabbit.

9. Finally, teen marriage failure may become a kind of self-fulfilling prophecy. That is, the couple and those close to them are aware that teen marriages fail much more often. Knowing that, they may put forth less effort to keep such a marriage from failing.

On the other hand, knowledge of the dangers of early marriage may have just the reverse effect. The couple may see the handicap as a challenge. They may set out to prove to themselves and others that their decision to marry young was a smart one. They may get stubborn and refuse to give up. They want to show the world that, in the words of a song made popular by Nat King Cole, "We were not too young at all."[19] More power to them! But it's a risky gamble.

## A Call to Caution

So persons who marry in their teens are just asking for trouble. They assume a terribly high risk of failure. In spite of that, large numbers of U.S. marriages involve a teenage girl.

Don't be in a rush to marry. There's a mountain of evidence showing it's unwise. To marry too early is like spitting in a tiger's face. You may get by with it. A few do. But don't count on it. The odds are against you.

Ask yourself the question, "Would I choose the same kind of marriage partner at age 25 that I would as a teenager?" Chances are you would not. Studies show that as American youths get older their views toward love grow more realistic.[20]

We could not in every case advise, "When in doubt, don't." That dictum would be too rigid and harsh. There may be special factors in a given case—though you should not just assume that you're an exception to the rule.

What we do suggest is this: "When in doubt, delay!" Take your time—*lots* of time. Tread water for a while. See what the passing of time does to your relationship. Does delay tear it apart? Or does time let it blossom and become more beautiful?

Delay can be frustrating now. You may feel that you just can't wait to get married. But it may be well worth your while to hold off on your decision. After all, if your choice is sound, you have a lifetime to reap the rewards. But if your choice goes sour, the harvest holds little but regrets.

## When Rapture Turns to Rupture

Marriages, like nuclear bombs, produce a great deal of fallout when they explode. There is often a long period of bitter bickering before the break. Marital problems affect the couple's social life and their work. Both mates and their children experience a great deal of emotional (and in some cases physical) pain. This spills over and affects most of the people close to them.

You may hear a lot about rational, sensible divorces. Why can't people go merrily on their separate ways with no regrets and no scars? It sounds right and reasonable. In practice it almost never happens.

## Divorce Starts a Nearly Endless Circle

Marriage failures seem to beget more and more failures. Divorces—like good marriages—tend to run in families. If you have grown up in a family where both parents were very happy with their marriage, your views toward marriage will tend to be positive. That is one of the very best assets you can bring to your own marriage.[21]

Girls who grow up in homes where there has been divorce need to be extra careful. Bert Adams found that daughters ". . . from intact families are more positive toward marriage and have the least sexual experience, while those from remarried families are most accepting of divorce and have more sexual experience." [22]

Other factors of your past home life will also affect your own chances of marital success. You are far more likely to have a good marriage if (in order of importance):

- Your parents are happy in their marriage.
- You had a happy childhood.
- There was a lack of conflict with your mother.
- Your home discipline was firm but not harsh.
- You had a strong attachment to your mother.
- You had a strong attachment to your father.
- There was a lack of conflict with your father.
- Your parents were frank with you about sex.
- Your childhood punishment was infrequent and mild.
- You have an expectant, positive attitude toward sex that is free from disgust or distaste. [23]

## Can the "Inevitable" Be Changed?

Does all this mean that you cannot build a good marriage if most or all of these family background factors are against you? Certainly not. Even if all of them are negative, you may well be able to turn the odds around. But you will have to work harder to make sure yours is a good marriage. And you will have to be even more careful than most people to make sure that your mate choice is a good one.

## The Great American *Marry*-Go-Round

The pattern of having many marriages and divorces during one's life is often identified with certain Hollywood and TV stars. I call these unions "revolving-door marriages." They constitute the great American marry-go-round. Persons who practice this pattern have several spouses—one at a time. A spouse is looked on in somewhat the same category as an automobile. You use it until the novelty wears thin. Then you trade it in for a fresh model.

It is of some interest to compare this type of revolving-door marriage to the current trend of just living together. In reality, this trend is another type of marry-go-round, a revolving-door "marriage" without legal papers. Couples who live together take a "let's try it out first" attitude. But the motives of the two sexes for living-in are quite different.

## Mattress Hoppers

At Ohio State University a study was made of couples who were living together. The study spanned three different time periods. One goal was to detect trends.

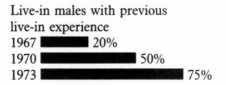

Live-in males with previous
live-in experience
1967 ▮▮▮ 20%
1970 ▮▮▮▮▮▮ 50%
1973 ▮▮▮▮▮▮▮▮ 75%

In only six years the number of live-in males who had formerly lived with at least one other female rose from 20 to 75%! That's a huge jump of 267%! Scientists rarely find such a rapid change in any type of social behavior.[24]

It appears that—at least early on—the men have more and more engaged in what I call "mattress hopping." They've moved from one bed partner to another—with little or no intention of wedding any one of them. It still happens. Glick and Spanier found that for only about 37% of the men with one experience in cohabitation and one marriage, did cohabitation lead to marriage. Thus in about

63% of the cases, cohabitation did not lead to ". . . marriage to the same person."[25] Recently, in the space of just one month I spoke with four women who had been used in just that way. Each of them separately vowed: No more sex without commitment! They learned the hard way.

## Living Together—for What?

The differing intentions of men and women in living-in arrangements were shown clearly in a Boulder study. There the most frequent reason the women gave for living together was that they were looking toward marriage. But the men? You guessed it. Their most frequent motive was simply sexual convenience and pleasure. One male put it very bluntly: "If you're living with a chick, it's a lot easier to get laid!" Well, that takes care of her hopes of marrying him!

Small wonder that one of the most common complaints of live-in women is, "I sometimes get the feeling I'm being used."[26] Well, there just may be a reason for that. Many men seem to feel, "Why marry her if I can get all the advantages of marriage without taking any of the responsibility?" (The version of that when I was young was: "Why buy the cow if you can get the milk free?") Why, indeed? That's something for young women to think about—a long, long time.

It's difficult to see how this mattress-hopper pattern is much different from revolving-door marriages. Of course, it's a lot easier to duck out of a live-in situation—no lawyers, no alimony (although at times "palimony"),[27] and, alas, no sense of responsibility. But there may be just as many tears and broken hearts.

By the way, women who live-in tend to be less educated, less religious, lower class, from one-parent homes, more sexually active and at earlier ages, have unstable relationships, lack legal rights, and have lower status jobs, less happy marriages, and parental disapproval.[28]

# ... **3** ........

# Pinpointing the Puzzlement

*W*HY is it so hard to tell the difference between a real love and mere romantic infatuation? Why does this problem leave so many people perplexed?

All of us must ask ourselves a tough question: Will my marriage turn out to be a success—or a sad statistic? Chances are that you will not be able to detect real love, if and when you find it. But why not?

The tragic truth is that your culture—past and present—has just plain failed you. In our Western society we tend to put much stress on the place of love in marriage. Yet for the most part, you have been denied the proper tools to help you recognize what real love is. Some of the things we call "love" have been with us for ages. Let's look at a few examples.

## There Was Confusion Then . . .

In the 12th century B.C., Israel's King David became lustfully enamored of Bathsheba as he watched her bathe. She was the wife of one of his soldiers who happened to be out of town at that time. David promptly proceeded to take her off to his own bed. (No kicking or screaming on her part is reported.)

Then there was the famed undying love of the old Hebrew prophet Hosea for his faithless wife Gomer. She had left his bed and board to become a harlot. That sad saga took place some 2,700 years ago.

Medieval upper-class married women at times had highly romantic affairs with men other than their own husbands. Sometimes they let their "lovers" undress them completely and lie with them in bed, bare as Mother Hubbard's cupboard. But it was understood that there was to be no hanky-pank! Intercourse was clearly a no-no. It was supposedly never to be a part of such romantic encounters. (At least that's the story that got passed down to us.)[1]

From these brief snatches of history we can readily see that the word *love* has been used to describe all kinds of quite different things. Compare the patient devotion Hosea had for his undeserving wife to the "lust at first sight" feelings displayed by King David.

There's a world of difference between the two, isn't there? To use the single word *love* to describe such diverse human emotions has to be troublesome.

## . . . And Confusion Now

The meaning of *love* is still being much confused. It may be even worse now than it used to be. Although most Americans want a marriage based on love, society has failed to help us detect real love. That failure has contributed to our high rates of divorce and loss of faith in marriage.

Yet each time you get those stars in your eyes, you will need to decide if it's real love. Unless you can do that, and do it better than most people have in the past, you too will be stuck with those frightful one-in-three odds. And that is too chancy a choice. You deserve a better break.

Not only do most of us want love, we need it as well. The slogan, "even dirty old men need love," expresses a truth. (And so do dirty old women and dirty little kids!) Every one of us needs at least one other person who really cares about us. We need someone who shares our hopes and joys, our sorrows and concerns. We need someone who honestly wants us to be our whole selves, to be fully fulfilled. We want someone to cry when we die—and really mean it.

We also need to give love. We need to have some other person on whom we can lavish our own caring and sharing.

This human need for love and companionship helps explain why youths in every generation cling doggedly to the hope of finding some loving and lovable life mate. Despite the current frightening odds against marital success, we sense that life yields its maximum meaning and its finest fulfillment with a true love mate. We yearn to find someone with whom we can share the depths of our inner being. You can find that kind of love in a good marriage.

This is the American marriage dream. It seems so right to most of us. Why then does it often go so wrong? The blame lies in part at least on the failure of our culture to help us distinguish true love from false love.

It is bad enough that society has not come up with adequate answers on mate choice. But it has done even worse than that. It has dished out false and misleading views of what love is and how it can be detected. It has done more to confuse the issue than to clarify it. The results have been marital chaos.

## Muddle in the Media

No themes are more popular in the public media than love and sex. Clever ad writers know that love and sex are among our deep desires and needs, so they exploit these to the hilt. They use sex to sell us soap and soup and salt and sugar—everything from gentle laxatives to zingy soda pop. Near nudes in a host of suggestive poses are dragged in quick succession across our field of awareness.

TV soap operas are literally littered with "romantic love." Mary loves John, who loves his file clerk, who's in love with her doctor, who loves—of all people—his wife. Many movies and books center around love stories. And what about popular songs? Does any other word appear in the titles and lyrics half as often as *love*? Young and old alike are bombarded from morn 'til night with love, love, and more love. Why then doesn't every single one of us know precisely and without fail what love is?

That answer is not hard to find. These media have simply deceived us. They use the term *love* a great deal, but they are almost always referring to romantic infatuation. They're not talking about love at all! As a result, few know what love really is.

What is supposed to happen when the time comes for you to wed? Somehow, just out of the clear blue, you're suddenly supposed to be able to ignore all the romantic rot you've been spoon-fed for years. By some miracle of magic you're supposed to know what love really is and come up with a good mate.

The wonder is not that so many of our marriages fail, but that so many manage somehow to survive.

## Unmasking the Media Myth

What is this false product that the media is always trying to peddle? The pattern of "media love" follows a fairly set sequence.

They meet, lights flash, they fall helplessly and hopelessly in love. Obstacles arise, but all barriers fall in the face of their great and marvelous love. Finally, they marry and live happily ever after. How sweet!

But hold on just a minute. That last phrase sounds strangely familiar. Isn't that the way fairy tales are supposed to end? You bet it is. And that's exactly what the romantic media myth is—a great big fairy tale. Sad to say, that suggested scenario seldom works out in real life. The actual path of "romantic love" tends to be quite different.

Wendell Johnson years ago called romantic love the "IFD disease." First, the other person is *Idealized*, and so is the situation the couple find themselves in. Since the ideals they dream about cannot become real, this brings on *Frustration*. That leads in turn to a loss of heart and morale, which then ends in Despair.[2] That's a far cry from what the media myth dream is supposed to be like.

## Failure of Religion

Our Judeo–Christian heritage has, like the media, let us down regarding the nature of love. Religion has not made clear to us love's multiple meanings. The problem goes back to the Hebrew and Greek languages in which the Old and New Testaments were recorded.

In *Sex and Love in the Bible*, William Cole made this important point:

The Old Testament uses the same word, *aheb* . . . to denote the love of God and the love of man. A similar economy of words prevails in the realm of human love, where the one verb and its [derivatives] refer not only to man's love for God but also his love for neighbor, including sensual love for members of the opposite sex.[3]

Now that's a wide span of meanings for just one, small, four-letter word! If that one word had all those meanings, how were even the translators to know in each case which kind of love the writers were talking about?

Now what about the New Testament? Its track record on clarifying love seems no better, but here the problem is just reversed. The confusion is not, as in the Old Testament, that one root word means many things. The problem is rather that a number of Greek words, each of which had its own unique shades of meaning, were at times all translated into the English as simply "love." That is, those many Greek meanings were all lumped together into just one English word.

Those many shades of different meanings served a very useful purpose for the Greeks. They helped the Greeks to sort out just what kind of love was under discussion. Such shades of meaning also must be a great help to the Greek scholars of today. But our Bible translators gave us no such wealth of words and meanings. All we can do is try our best to guess which kind of love the Bible writers had in mind each time the word is used.

Let's take a brief look at each of the five Greek words for "love."

*1. Sensual love.* This is sexual desire. Greeks called it *epithymia*.

*2. Yearning for unity.* For the Greeks this meant a drive to unite with something attractive. They called it *eros*. Our English word *erotic* means passion and sex, but for the Greeks, *eros* had a much broader meaning. It could even be used to describe love for God. C. S. Lewis uses the word to mean "falling in love."[4]

3. *Brotherly love.* This is the kind of love shared by good friends and companions. It is a close feeling that develops when two persons have many things in common. The Greek word for this is *philia.*

4. *Family affection.* This is the kind of love shared by parents and children. The Greeks called this *storge.*

5. *Self-giving love.* Greek Christians invented this concept and called it *agape.* They associated this type of love with Jesus. It is the self-giving devotion to others regardless of their merits. There are some people you don't think are very lovable, but you can love them anyway, simply because they are human beings. Or as both Judaism and Christianity hold, God created every human being in God's own image. And even if persons have nothing else going for them, that's enough. They thereby deserve our caring concern for their well-being.

## Guessing at Meanings

Clearly, each one of these five words used by the Greeks has its own distinct meaning. Each is quite different from all the rest. Yet in most of our Bibles, both Catholic and Protestant, all five Greek words are translated into just one English word—*love.* That gives us no clue as to the original thought. Bible readers who don't know Greek are left with a hopeless task. Each time we come upon the word *love,* we must try to figure out the content from the context.

In this sense, then, our religion has indeed failed us. Obscurity in the Scriptures and muddle in the media leave us confused as to what love is all about. Is love sexual attraction or friendly fondness or brotherly affection?

When all these meanings get loaded onto just one word, the result is hopeless confusion. No wonder we have a hard time deciding when we've found true love.

## Real Love Includes All Five

A good marriage will likely need to have every one of these five types of love—and have them in healthy helpings.

*1. Strong sex interest.* Hornell Hart used to tell his classes at Duke that three things had to be true for the human race to survive. We had to (a) get our breakfast, (b) avoid being someone else's breakfast, and (c) have at least a passing interest in sex.

Well, for most of us, interest in sex is a trifle more than passing. Couples normally do have strong erotic feelings for each other. A good marriage includes mutual joy and satisfaction in sex.

Yet it is quite possible to give sex an importance far beyond what it deserves. As a youth, I was told by a Ph.D. from Yale that "good sex is 85% of a good marriage." That was and still is utter nonsense. Any Ph.D., and certainly one from Yale, should know better. Sex is important, but it is only one of many very important parts of a good relationship.

*2. Respect and admiration.* Couples need to have a strong mutual attraction and hold each other in high regard.

*3. Friendship and fellowship.* Couples also need to be true comrades. They need to have many things in common—the more the better. They must like each other a lot, and be the best of friends.

*4. Affection.* And, of course, there must be tender feelings. Each partner should provide the other with a haven of refuge from harsh attacks in the outside world. We all need sympathy and empathy to soothe our hurts. We need to be understood. Love can mean a shoulder to cry on when our burdens are too heavy to bear alone.

*5. Self-giving devotion.* Finally, a good marriage has to have a good deal of *agape* love. All of us have some unlovable traits. A spouse must at times love not because of, but in spite of, the other person's faults. You will have to love your mate even during those times when you feel he or she does not deserve it. Like you, your spouse may sometimes not be very lovable. Your mate may at times be cranky, or lose their temper, or be depressed, or not want to talk to you. That will take some *agape* love on your part.

A good marriage will have a heavy sprinkling of every one of these kinds of love. More than that, no one of them (with the possible exception of friendship) is enough in itself to build and sustain a healthy marriage. A balance of all five is a much better bet.

## The Failure of Social Science—a Professional Pussyfoot

We might well expect that the social sciences would be of most help with this problem of love. Researchers have made many kinds of studies about dating and mating over the years. Since the number one courtship query of youth is, "How can I know if it's love?" Isn't it logical to assume that this issue should have had prime time with the social researchers? It may seem logical, but it doesn't happen to be true.

## From the "Brains": Disdain

The hard fact is that in this century there has been only one book that has given fairly full treatment to this subject: *Of Love and Lust* by Theodor Reik.[5] And even this excellent book has some serious drawbacks. It has more than 600 pages (which would turn off most young readers) and it is full of technical medical terms. With the dearth of useful data on love, no wonder so many people are confused about how to detect the real thing. We social scientists have failed to cope with this critical need. Like religion and the media, science has largely failed to help us recognize love.

## Compounding the Confusion: Certain Symptoms Seem Similar

One further factor makes it hard for you to know if you're really in love. Many of the same romantic symptoms occur in *both* love and infatuation. It's important for you to know what these similar symptoms are.

*Powerful pull to passion.* You may think that if you have strong sexual feelings toward another person, you must surely be in love. That is far from the truth. Sex attraction can exist without love. Indeed, you may feel passionate toward a person you've not met. Their picture, their appearance on the stage or on the screen, or mere daydreams may be quite enough to arouse your sex interest.

If you like a member of the opposite sex well enough to want to be with them a lot, don't be surprised if you feel a good deal of sex interest too. If you engage in a lot of necking and petting, sex feelings may become highly urgent. Sex may even become the most prominent part of your relationship. But even that kind of desire does not mean your love is real. Sexual urges can be just as strong in false love as in true love.

*Gnawing need for nearness.* As it is with sex interest, so it is with the deep desire to be together. It can be present in infatuation just as in love. You may want to be together almost all the time. If you are parted for even a few hours you will have a feeling of emptiness, a deep longing for each other. Does this mean you have real love in your relationship? Not at all. Such longing can be as much present in false love as it is in the real thing.

*Funny feelings.* Getting strange feelings "in the middle" when you see or think about another person is not in itself a valid clue. That happens in pseudo-love every bit as much as it does in real love.

You may feel like you're walking on clouds. As long as things go well between you, your joy knows no bounds. That you "have each other" is quite enough—nothing else seems to matter.

But when things go wrong between you, your misery is equally strong. You have a hollow feeling in the pit of your stomach. You long for things to be right again between you. Your pride may not let you show your feelings openly, but you'd give almost anything if you two could again be the same as you were before.

So that must mean you love each other very much, right? Dead wrong. It can happen just like that in infatuation, every bit as much as with love. Such feelings are perhaps even more likely in infatuation.

A pull to passion, the need for nearness, and funny feelings—these three clues are romantic fool's gold. Like a greenhorn prospector, you may get all excited in the firm belief that you've struck it rich in the mine of love. But the greenhorn prospector mistook pyrite for gold, and you may mistake infatuation for true love. You may have strong sex feelings, a need for nearness, and a host of strange new emotions. But don't trust such clues. They may be romantic fool's gold.

To detect pyrite there is one simple test. Just pop it into a pan and put it on a hot stove. If it's real gold, it won't be damaged. But fool's gold will sizzle and smoke and send out a strong stench. Sad to say, there's no such simple test to detect romantic fool's gold. You can scarcely put your beloved in a hot pan—at least not for very long!

All of this may lead you to conclude that no help is to be had with this problem. That is not true. But you do need to keep two things clearly in mind. First, look for more valid clues than the three described above. Second, go slowly.

## WANTED: A Love That Lasts

All of this is indeed discouraging. It is almost as if your culture has conspired against you. It has laid down rigid rules defining high goals for marriage success. Then it has built roadblocks that tend to keep you from reaching those goals. Yet the awful fact remains—you must try to predict in advance whether your choice of a mate will be a wise one. It is one of the most important decisions you will ever have to make.

It is no wonder that thoughtful young people become anxious about this choice. But don't despair—you *can* determine whether it's real love or a mere infatuation. Science can help.

There are 14 simple clues you can use to test a relationship. Taken together, these clues will tell you whether it's genuine love. Furthermore, you can easily use 13 of these clues in your own situation, and you can do it all by yourself—during the romance.

Just ask yourself each of the 14 key questions that appear in the following chapters.[6] Then carefully think about how the traits for each of these clues seem to apply to your specific case. Finally, based on an honest, unbiased assessment of the total results, determine the degree to which real love seems to be indicated for your romance.

## Three Precautions

Before you look at the 14 clues, please note three warnings:

*1. The order is not important.* Just because a clue comes early in the list, you should not assume it is of more value than clues listed later. It is not. The clues are not arranged from high to low, or low to high.

2. *No clue can stand alone.* No one of the clues is of itself a sound basis on which to make a decision. Even four or five are not enough. It would be a big mistake to act rashly. In fact, every one of those clues is very important. Otherwise, it wouldn't be in the list at all.

One young woman, soon after hearing the 14 points explained in class, came by my office. "Prof," she announced, "I broke up with my boyfriend last night."

"You did? Why did you do that?" I asked.

"Well number seven hit us right between the eyes!"

Well, maybe it did. But just because one or two of the clues seem to point to romantic infatuation instead of love, that is no cause to call it quits. That would be a gross misuse of the 14 clues.

There may well be no such thing as "pure love" or "pure infatuation." Your relationship is much more likely to be a mixture of both. So you need to look beyond what is indicated by any one clue. You need to find out what the whole pattern of all the clues seems to show. Ask yourself: "Into which category do *most* of the traits in this relationship seem to fall?" Can you honestly say that a large majority of the 14 clues do indeed fall into the real love column? If not, you can assume that you don't yet have enough love to consider marriage. Give your relationship more time, then test it again with the clues. See if it grows more and more into love as time goes by. To qualify as a reasonably valid love, you need good scores on at least 11 or 12 of the 14 clues. Anything less would be a flimsy foundation for marriage.

3. *One-sided loves won't work.* Real love can never be a one-way street. Love must be mutual. No matter how solid you feel your own love is, the other person must

love you in return. Otherwise there is bound to be trouble ahead.

A young woman once admitted to me that she knew her young man didn't really love her. Yet she kept pressing him to marry her. "Just give us a year of marriage and I'll make him love me," she declared. She'd better not count on that. Most people are pretty much the same after marriage as before. There's no magic in a marriage license. If there's any reforming to be done, it had best be done *before,* not after, the wedding. And make very sure that the change is for keeps. Consistent action is called for, not mere promises.

# ... 4 .......

## CLUE ONE:
## What Is the
## Major Attraction?

*W*HAT is your main interest in the other person? What appeals to you most? What "turns you on"? Your answers to these questions can help you decide if it's love.

### Signs of Infatuation

If you are infatuated, *your main interest is likely to be the other person's physical equipment.* For males, that probably translates into whether the woman has a pretty face and nice curves in all the right places. Attractive eyes and an athletic body may really get a female's attention. When girls sigh, "Oooh! What a hunk!" or boys exclaim, "Get a load of that!" they don't mean the other person has a bright brain, do they?

All of that suggests infatuation. The main stress is on things you can perceive right away—what you can see, hear, smell, taste, or touch about the person.

## Signs of Love

If you truly love someone, on the other hand, *your interest is in his or her total personality.* You're attracted to the whole person. The physical features are only some of the many things you like. It's not just the body you care about, it's what's housed *in* the body. It's not just what shows on the surface, but also what's beneath the surface. The face, after all, is just a mask. It's what's behind the mask that counts most. Real love arms you with X-ray vision—you can see far more about the one you love than what first meets the eye. And that's all to the good.

People today have a great way of making this point. They say, "You're a beautiful person." Now, they don't mean by that that you'd win a beauty contest. You may have a face that would stop a clock! What they mean is that you're a beautiful *kind* of person—nice to be around. Whether or not you *look* beautiful, you *are* beautiful.

You'll want to keep this distinction clearly in mind in the search for love. Some men make a tragic mistake— they pass up a beautiful woman to marry a pretty girl. But looks can be deceiving. A beautiful face and a handsome body are like the wrapping around a gift. The outside glitter tells you nothing at all about what's inside. Any old thing can be done up in a nice wrapping, yet the contents may be something you won't like at all. In fact, a gift box may be completely empty—and so may a pretty face or a handsome head!

Out of the dozens of high school assemblies I went to as a boy, I recall only one. "Boys," the speaker said solemnly, "before you marry a girl for her pretty face and sexy form, ask yourself: What's she going to look like in 30 years?" That stopped me. And it should stop you, too.

Indeed, what *will* she/he look like in 30 years? She'll no doubt have her share of wrinkles and unsightly sags and bags. He may sport a shiny bald head where that lush crop of curls now hangs. And his Greek-god chest? It may well have slipped down about a foot. Probably neither of you will look like too much by then. In spite of that, you'll be expected to remain married. And if you're to do that, you'll need more going for you than a few faded memories of how pretty or how handsome each of you *used* to look.

## What if You Marry for Sex?

Strong physical attraction is normally tied to sex interest. But even if a couple's sex life is the very best, that isn't enough. A marriage based only on sex attraction will last no more than three to five years.

Consider a few solid facts of life before you marry for sex. For instance, do you know how often the typical American married couple has sex during an average week? The answer is two or three times (that's per week, not per night!). And do you know how long the average American married couple spends in sexual intercourse each time? It's just eight minutes—and that includes all the foreplay and afterglow! They spend only four to five minutes in actual penetration.[1]

Indeed, the above-cited figures may be too high. A just-released University of Chicago study of 1500 adults puts the average amount of sex at once per week! And happily married couples had sex the most often—about 1½ times a week.[2] Further, compared to similar data from 1979, young men seem to have lower levels of sexual activity today, with fewer sexual contacts and fewer partners.[3]

Some say these numbers are a sad commentary on American sex life. Be that as it may, it's clear that we devote very little time to sex. Let's add up the total. (We'll take the larger figures. We don't want anyone to feel cheated!)

Number of times per week        3
Number of minutes per time      8

Grand total                    24  minutes per week

Just think about that! There are 168 hours in a week—and the average couple spends less than half an hour of that time having sex! *Question: If you marry mainly for sex, what in the world are you going to do the rest of the time?* Now, you're going to spend more time looking at each other across the breakfast table (curlers, whiskers, and all) than you'll spend copulating in bed. So you'd just better have something worthwhile to talk about. No matter how torrid that half hour of sex might be, life can get mighty dull the rest of the time. Please take note: good sex will never save a bad marriage.[4]

Some erotic interest in members of the opposite sex is of course to be expected during most of our lives. The story goes that an aging Supreme Court justice once spotted a shapely young woman undulating down the walk. He stared for a few moments, with never the slightest show of shame. Turning to an aide he sighed, "Ah! Would that I were a man of 60 again!" The old codger may have been aging in body, but he had some pretty young ideas. Sex interest can continue even into old age.

It's quite normal for us to feel physical attraction, be it in the context of love or infatuation or just that fleeting "instant urge." The key is how much importance such feelings have in a total relationship. In infatuation, the other's body is the major interest. In love, it is but one of many things that attract.

## . . . **5** . . . . . . .

# CLUE TWO:
# How Many
# Factors Attract?

*H* ow many things about the person attract you?
Your answer can help you know whether your
feelings are real love.

Think of as many things as you can that you really like
about him or her. Jot them down in a list. Include such
things as the way a person acts, thinks, feels, and looks.
What about life goals? Hobbies? Habits? Religion? Favorite interests? Motives and ambitions?

When the list is fairly complete, go through it and do
three things. First, place a check beside just those things
that you find *really* attractive about the person, traits that
you very much like and admire.

Second, underline those factors that you and the other
person share as interests. Do you think alike, feel the
same, react pro and con to the same things? What things
do you disagree on—even clash about? Draw a circle
around those.

Finally, ask yourself why you are interested in those
shared attractions. Were you interested in them *before* you
met him or her? If you took an interest in golf or skating

only after you found your friend liked it, your interest may not be genuine and lasting.

Take for instance the matter of religion. Suppose one of you grew up Methodist, the other Roman Catholic. You both feel you want religion to play a vital part in your home. Let's say the Protestant is persuaded to switch rather than fight—so as to keep religious peace in the family. Does that mean the matter is all settled? Probably not. While the chances for success of such mixed marriages have improved in recent years, the track record is still far from encouraging. Several studies show that Catholic–Protestant unions fail much more often than those where partners have had the same religious background.[1]

And Christian/non-Christian marriages are even more risky.

Ask this question: Would you adopt the other person's religion by your own choice even if you two were to break up? If the answer is no, you'd best beware. Interests you have or actions you take because of the other are not likely to last. Once married, you may lose your enthusiasm for such arrangements with frightening speed. On the other hand, interests that each of you had before you met are quite certain to stay with you, together or not.

## Signs of Infatuation

In an infatuation *the number of factors that attract you are relatively few.* He may be very much struck by her lovely hair, her pretty legs, her bubbly laugh. She is very fond of his nice smile, his teasing sense of humor, the way he walks. And that's about the size of it. Just a few things attract.

However, those few things that do attract may seem *very* enticing. He may think she has the softest hair he's ever run his fingers through. Her legs are the prettiest he's ever seen, her laugh is utterly delightful. His smile may just melt her heart, and his jaunty walk thrills her no end. She can't resist laughing at his clever quips and jokes. Some things about the other really "send" you.

Still, the truth remains—only a few things attract you to the person. Bad news. What about all those dozens of other personality traits the person has? Maybe you haven't really thought much about those. You've been preoccupied with the things you do find attractive.

You've ignored the others. Do you think that those other things can just wait until later? Do they seem unimportant? Alas, that means that you're just infatuated.

Those other things will indeed be *very* important. Lots of shared factors will help cement your love more and more. But those differences will grow. Those you'll just have to put up with—and for years to come.

## Signs of Love

If it's love, *many or most qualities of the person—and the relationship—attract you.* You like not only the way the person looks and talks, but the way he or she thinks and feels about things and other people. Do you like the person's reactions to personal success? To failure? To tough challenges? To faults in his or her self, and in you or others? What about use of leisure time? And what about thoughtfulness, kindness, courage, temper, and temperament? Does the person have healthy and balanced attitudes toward money, sex, school, family, and friends? Toward the past and the future? What about bad habits?

Each of us has a multitude of traits, emotions, ideas, and attitudes. An individual personality has many different sides. So ask yourself two questions. (1) How many of the countless traits of this person do I know enough about? (2) How many of those things do I find attractive? If you don't know very much about the person, you can't judge the relationship. You need time and effort so you get to know him or her extremely well. Only then can you judge your reaction to the many, many facets of that person's nature. If many or most of those factors attract you, this tends to indicate real love. When the excitement and romance wear off in a marriage, you need lots of other interests in common to hold you together over the long pull. You need to *like* each other as well as *love* each other.

The interests you do have in common need to be important rather than trivial. It doesn't matter much that you like the same kind of pizzas and movies. It matters very much whether you agree on life-style and whether you want to have children, make lots of money, or have two separate careers. And do the interests you share depend on some special setting—a bowling alley, movie theater, skating rink, a high mountain? Or can you do most things that interest you anywhere and still enjoy each other?

Also consider how similar your backgrounds have been. Do the two of you come from the same type of family and social class? Do you have similar religions, political views, goals, and aspirations? The more things you have in common, the more likely you are to have the kind of foundation that can support the growth of real love.

Unexciting as it may sound, one of the best prospects for a good marriage is the boy or girl next door. You grow up with each other, play together as children, and go to school together. You get to know each other extremely well. And your family and social backgrounds are probably pretty much alike. That's all in your favor when it comes to adjusting to marriage.

## Do Opposites Really Attract?

Two persons who are *psychological* opposites may attract and have a good marriage. *Social* opposites almost never do.

For example, a person who has a psychological need to dominate other people may be quite content with a mate who likes to be dominated. Their differences tend to complement each other and bring each of them psychic satisfaction. Their seemingly happy state will last, however, only as long as the less dominant partner is willing to submit. If he or she ever balks at such an arrangement, the sparks will begin to fly.

Though in some cases a couple may be psychological opposites and get along fine, social opposites are quite another matter. The greater the social differences, the greater the dangers. In fairy tales we read that a prince marries a scrub girl and they live happily ever after. In real life it seldom happens. Make sure you are on the same social wavelength before you commit yourselves to marry. Talk over a wide range of subjects and share ideas and backgrounds. Include things like:

*Roots.* How similar are you as to: Social class? Racial, national, and ethnic roots? City vs. country backgrounds? Religions?

*Values.* What is very important to you: Religion? Money? Social position and acceptance? Prestige? Sex before/after marriage? Who decides?

*Children.* Do you like them? Want them? How many? What about birth control? If so, what kind? Who's responsible for it?

*Money.* How much is enough? Who will make it? Save it? For what? Spend it? On what? Who'll budget, pay bills, do the shopping? (More married couples fight about money than any other thing.)

*Sex roles.* Who'll make decisions? Will both work? Will you share home chores? If babies come, will the wife work outside the home?

*Where and how to live.* Region? Rural or urban? Fancy or modest?

*Main interests.* Hobbies? Vocation plans? Education? Recreation likes and dislikes?

*Investment in your future.* What do you plan to do about war, pollution, poverty, and so on?

*Concepts of marriage.* For keeps? Trust and fidelity? Companionship?

*Major goals and hopes for the future.* What do you want out of life? How will you get there from here? Who can help?

The more you agree on these and other key issues, the better your chances for success in marriage. You need to be friends as well as lovers. If you have too many opposites, that will *de*tract, not *at*tract. We all tend to like (and to like to be with) persons who agree with us on most things rather than those who do not. If you can share at many levels—ideas, activities, sentiments, goals—your marriage will wear well. If not, it will "wear out."

## Can You Talk and Adapt?

So you think you've found an angel? You haven't. Angels in this level of life are mighty hard to come by.

No matter how compatible you are, your marriage will not be free of conflict. So your ability to adapt and adjust is of prime importance. Can the two of you work out differences? Can you talk over problems with honesty? Can you solve disputes without hurting each other? Do either of you get mad or get grumpy when things don't go your way? Do you feel free to share your true feelings, or do you hold back out of fear or lack of trust and confidence? You'd best find out *before* you marry.

It is not enough just to be able to communicate. Even couples who fight a lot are communicating, but in all the wrong ways. The essential thing is that you be able to work out constructive solutions to problems together, that you develop skills to work through conflict in creative ways. That gives you a great advantage when you have to face adjustments and make decisions in your marriage.

## Doesn't Familiarity Breed Contempt?

Folklore has long made that claim, but it's not true if a couple is well matched. If you two have few things in common and marry on the basis of surface attractions, then getting to know each other better may indeed lead to contempt. The more you know, the less you like each other.

But if you have many factors that attract and take time to know each other well *before* marriage, the opposite will be true. Then, as Zick Rubin suggests, "familiarity breeds *content*," not contempt.[2]

## · · · **6** · · · · · · · ·

# CLUE THREE:
# How Did
# It Start?

*T* HINK back to when it all began. Did you feel that you knew right away that "he (or she) is for me"? Or did your interest grow over a long period of time? How long did it take for your "love" to come into full bloom? Your answer to such questions can tell you a lot about whether your romance is real love.

### Signs of Infatuation

Infatuation *tends to start fast.* You know the story: eyes meet across a crowded room—and they know!

Well, bless their hearts! They don't know *anything*— except that they have a good first impression of each other. They like what appears on the surface. They are pleased by what they can discover about each other right away. They have a warm, glowing feeling of being "at home" in each other's presence. But no one can possibly know if it is real love based only on brief acquaintance.

## What about "Love at First Sight"?

If there is one thing the science of marriage is quite clear about, it is this. There is no such thing as love at first sight.

A human personality is much too complex to permit that kind of instant insight. Your senses show you only the superficial, the shallow shell. Real love requires that you know and like the other person's whole self. You need to understand the full array of complex traits that lie hidden deep within the person. You are not going to discover all that through quick, casual contacts.

On top of that, you need to figure out whether those many facets of both your personalities will fit together well. You can't find that out in a few minutes, or even a few weeks. It will take months—maybe even years.

## Signs of Love

The evidence is clear. Love *starts slowly*. It can't be any other way. Studies have shown that the longer the period of courtship and engagement, the better the chances for success in a marriage. There is no substitute for passing the test of time. A year is better than six months. Two years are better than one. Three years are better than two, four better than three, five better than four.

Do you exclaim in disbelief, "Five years!?" Yes, five years. The statistics are crystal clear.

Obviously you can't afford to spend five years exploring too many relationships. If you do, you may end up feeling feeble before you marry! But you certainly won't need five years to find out that most of your relationships are not for keeps. With some it won't take you five minutes.

But take as much time as you need to decide wisely. The longer the courtship, the better your chances for a good marriage. Remember, the odds of success are under 50-50. These days, no couple should enter the high privilege of marriage—and it is a high privilege—without at least two years of a good courtship and engagement. Anything less than that will be skating on thin ice.

"But hold on a minute, Prof," someone says. "My Uncle Jehosephat and Aunt Citronella had a whirlwind courtship. They met, fell in love, and were married all in the space of two months. They've been hitched now for over 30 years and they're as happy as two bugs in a rug. Now what do you say to *that?*"

I say: "Thank God, they lucked out!" It just so happened that they did have the seeds of a good match. But in the space of only eight or nine weeks they could not possibly have known that. They took one whale of a gamble. In this case, they won—but the odds were strongly against them.

Of course, time is not the only factor. It depends in part on what you do with that time. Maybe you meet, then after a few days together are separated for a long time. Though four years pass from the first kiss to the wedding day, you may have actually been together only a few short weeks. That is not enough. That does not pass the test of time.

The quality of the time spent with each other is as important as the quantity. People can be great actors. We all tend to play games with one another, to appear to be what we are not. A couple might date for a long period, yet have only a shallow knowledge of each other. You need to find out what the person is like way down deep inside, beneath the display-window mask.

For years I've made a bold half-tongue-in-cheek suggestion to students: "No couple should marry until they've spent at least one weekend camping out together—properly chaperoned, of course!" You may learn more from one campout than you can from a dozen dates where each of you is on your best behavior. Find out how he or she reacts to a tough problem.

Suppose it pours cold rain in the night. Someone forgot to trench around her tent. Water seeps up through her sleeping bag. She starts to squirm in discomfort. She gets up cold, wet, and hungry. But the matches got wet, so no heat and no breakfast. Take a good, long look at how she acts then. Does she lose her cool? or pout? Does she take it out on him?

And how about if he slips and falls while fishing, banging his tailbone on a rock? He gets doused in ice-cold water. He loses a big fish, and with it his favorite rod and reel. He comes in drenched and dripping. Look him over very closely.

Does he blame her for all his woes? Does he get mad and "cuss a blue streak" at his luck, or—worse yet—at her? Does he just clam up? Does he tease her when she's miserable, then grow angry when the ribbing is leveled at him?

Or can they roll with the punches and see the humor in their sad situation? Can they laugh at themselves? The way you react to problems like these will be a good clue to how you'll react to tough problems in marriage.

## The Age of Anxiety

Once you reach the late 20s the chances that you will marry within the next year grow less with each passing birthday. Many who reach this stage grow anxious. They may be tempted to marry just about anyone who comes along out of fear that they will not have a better offer.

One eager teacher on the verge of 30 met a young man at Duke summer school. After a whirlwind courtship of three weeks, they went to a nearby state and got married. It did not work out. It was a case of "marry in haste and repent in leisure."

You can feel very lonesome living alone, it's true. But you can also feel lonely and miserable living with your mate if you're not well matched. It's no fun to live with someone who doesn't understand and care for you. Better to stay single than to live in a marital hell.

## When Does It All Start?

If you're young, extra caution is in order. Studies show that the young are more likely to be infatuated than genuinely in love. So the younger you are, the more time you ought to take to decide. A good, long period of courtship will help you be sure that it's the real thing. Be very sure you pass that all-important "test of time."

## . . . **7** . . . . . . .

# CLUE FOUR:
# How Consistent Is
# Your Level of Interest?

*T* HE path of true love never runs smoothly." So goes an old American adage, and a lot of people take it at full face value. One couple even named their old car "Tru Luv"—since it, too, never ran smoothly.

Is this saying true? Or is it just one more example of how infatuation and love get all twisted around in the public mind? The degree to which a couple's interest in each other stays smooth and consistent can be a good clue to the nature of their romance.

### Signs of Infatuation

It is in fact infatuation rather than love that does not run smoothly. In an infatuation, *a couple's interest in each other comes and goes.*

If you are infatuated, your interest in the other will fluctuate. You are never quite sure one day how you will feel the next. Your interest may range from high peaks of certainty about your relationship and its future, to deep valleys of doubt. One day you may feel sure this is the right person for you. You think you might just as well set the wedding date. Then you develop doubts. You wonder if the two of you should date others for a while, to test your feelings more. But then things go better again and you become more confident. Your feelings seem to bounce back and forth. Feelings of uncertainty fit right in with what we've learned about romantic infatuation. If you're infatuated, you're attracted to only a few things about the other person—probably physical and surface traits. Your interest in each other grew rather fast. The roots of such a relationship are too thin to nourish it for long. The soil is too shallow to keep your interest in each other strong at all times, so your feelings are not consistent.

Sex may also be the reason for lack of consistent interest. If a couple becomes involved in pleasurable sex behavior, their interest in each other may vary more or less in direct proportion to the strength of their sex urge at any given time.

## Signs of Love

In real love *the relationship tends to even out.* It becomes more and more consistent. You can depend on your interest in each other staying pretty much the same over a long period of time. You feel comfortable with it, and with each other. If you don't reach the peaks of excitement so prevalent in infatuation, neither do you plunge to the depths. As time goes on, you come to count on your love. You know it will be there when you need it.

This is not to say that in real love there will be no problems to iron out, no hardships to work around, especially in the early stages of your courtship. Any two people will find some rough edges to smooth out when they start to reveal and merge the many facets of their complex inner selves. Problems of adjustment cannot be avoided. But the longer you know each other, the easier it is to cope when you have real love.

You will want to know with some certainty *before you marry* that the two of you have clearly achieved a close, happy, dependable degree of harmony and mutual fulfillment. The best way to predict the future is to study closely the evidence from the past and the experience of the present. If you had a good relationship all last week, and the week before that, and the month before that, then you are more likely to have it next week, next month, and the year after that. The longer you've had a consistent pattern in the past, the more certain you can be that you'll have it in the future. Time takes a lot of the guesswork out of your big decision.

As real love grows, you stabilize your feelings and actions toward each other. You learn to resolve tensions between you. It becomes easier to talk over and work out your differences. As James McCary says, "Mature love is evenly balanced and temperate. Where romantic love [infatuation] is hot, mature love is warm. Mature love is not an extreme, but a way of life."[1]

You might say that love is a kind of comfortable "warm fuzzy."

## ··· **8** ········

# CLUE FIVE: How Does It Affect Your Personality?

$T$ HE common belief is that when you "fall in love" you don't act at all like your normal self. You lose your appetite. You can't sleep. You forget things, neglect things, drop things, foul up things. You're moody. You daydream. You stumble over chairs and stairs. You can't study, can't work.

Can this really be love? Is love a state of being beyond reason and self-control? Wrong again. As the Disney movie *Bambi* put it, you're "twitterpated."

### Signs of Infatuation

It is romantic infatuation, not love, that has *a disorganizing and destructive effect on your personality*. Infatuation makes you less effective, less efficient, less your real self. People probably notice it right away.

"What's come over that kid?" Dad may explode. "She won't eat. She doesn't do her homework. She doesn't even hear when I talk to her. Is she sick?"

"Oh no," Mom says with a smile. "She's in love." No she isn't. She's just infatuated.

But Mom is scarcely alone in making this wrong assumption. Here, for example, is an excerpt from an article published in *Harper's Bazaar*.

> If you suddenly can't add up (when you always had straight A's in math) . . . or stand up on the ski slopes without his arm around you (although you were educated at [Aspen]) or shut up talking to him long distance—you're in love.[1]

Now doesn't that sound silly? But it's a pretty good description of romantic infatuation. The sad thing is that the article calls the condition "love," thus plunging headlong into the media myth trap.

Walking around in a daydream may seem quite harmless. But some of the results of infatuation are not so innocent. Robert Kelly noted that "immature love (infatuation) . . . is irresponsible and fails to consider the future consequences of today's actions."[2] In such a condition, you might well lose your head and do things you wouldn't otherwise think of doing. You may even foul up your whole life.

Theodor Reik cited the case of a girl who sought counseling. "I did not consider any more whether it was wrong or right to kiss him good night," she said. "It did not matter, nothing matters any more."[3] If you let yourself get so involved with someone that "nothing matters" except your romance, you could be exploited and deeply hurt. The risk is especially high if the feelings of love or infatuation are mainly on one side.

## The Principle of Least Interest

One-sided love or infatuation occurs quite often. Scientists who study this condition have come up with what they call the "principle of least interest." This principle states that in a one-sided romance, the partner who has the least interest in continuing the affair is able to control the other person. That's because the one who is more involved has more at stake.

No one should use another human being for selfish purposes, but people often do. A girl who doesn't care much for a boy may keep him dangling on a string. It may build up her ego to have someone care so much for her. Or he may be just a convenience—she can always count on him for a date if nobody else asks her. She knows he'll put up with shabby treatment because he's so emotionally involved. It's a mean trick, but some girls—and boys—do it.

Or the boy may be the one with the least interest in continuing the affair. If so, he may demand more sexual favors than his girlfriend wants to give. Since she fears he may leave her if she doesn't give in, she may yield just to try to hold him. Since he doesn't care very much for her, he may take advantage of her.

If a girl has to give a guy sex to keep him, she should certainly ask herself if such a fellow is worth keeping. If his main interest in her is sex, he'll probably drop her after a while anyway. On the other hand, if a boy really does love a girl, he won't press her to do things that he knows are against her principles. He'll respect her right to do what she feels she ought to do.

Real love is responsible and glad to assume the consequences of mutual acts. Infatuation, on the other hand, tends to dodge responsibility. So when a boy says to a girl, "If you loved me, you'd let me," her logical reply will be, "If you really loved me, you wouldn't ask me to." And he wouldn't, either.

## Signs of Love

Real love will have *an organizing and a constructive effect on your personality.* It brings out the best in you. As Hirning and Hirning wrote, "There is an intense and satisfying feeling of greater self-realization and expression, as well as a feeling of having one's own personality reinforced and strengthened and enriched." Duvall and Hill added that love gives you "new energy and ambition, and more interest in life. . . . It is creative, brings an eagerness to grow, to improve, to work for worthy purposes and ideals. Love is associated with feelings of self-confidence, trust and security."[4]

The person who loves makes an effort to be more deserving of the beloved. Two sisters were heard to agree that their older brother's wife is good for him. "Before he met Jane, he had few goals and not much direction in his life," said one. The other nodded. "When he married her, it really made a man out of him." Love gave him the will to improve himself. Love lifted him to new levels of maturity and responsible action. It will do the same for you.

If you love someone, you want your beloved to be proud of you, so you try harder. Life has more purpose. You make plans and save for the future. Life takes on new meaning, more sparkle. You may daydream a lot, but your thoughts center on plans that are not beyond your reach. And you have more energy. Love woos you to function at your highest level.

Here's a good test for students. If you're infatuated, your grades will go down. If you're in love, your grades will go up. You'll be better organized and more alert. (You may study less but enjoy it more!)

Your friends and teachers and parents may well notice the change for the good. They may comment, "My, since she's been going with him, she takes herself and her duties a lot more seriously." Or, "Have you noticed how much more dependable he is now?"

If you experience real love, you may find that your attitude toward all people and the whole of life has been elevated. "We have heard 'all the world loves a lover,' " noted Duvall and Hill. "The converse is also true, 'Lovers love all the world.' "[5] Love doesn't make you turn inward and isolate yourself and your beloved. On the contrary, as Judson T. and Mary Landis wrote:

> The man or woman who loves and is loved and accepted by one person can live and function in other relationships more effectively. He is free to be himself without defensiveness; he can worry less about protecting his ego from hurt. He can be more outgoing and confident in his relationships. People who love and are loved are not completely absorbed with love; they are more fully functioning personalities in all aspects of life. . . . It promotes growth and increases awareness of meanings, needs and opportunities in the world about one.[6]

What if you have loved and lost? You may have had a real love relationship that did not result in marriage. Perhaps one or both of you did not recognize at the time that it was real love. Or some tragedy may have robbed you of your beloved.

In spite of the pain of loss, you still are likely to be a better person for having had love. You can better understand yourself and be better prepared for finding success in your future relationships. You will be more mature. You grew through your love experience, and that growth will not all wither away. You will be more alert to find and hold some other love in the months and years to come.

Come what may, real love will have an organizing and constructive effect on your personality.

## • • • 9 • • • • • • •

# CLUE SIX:
# How and When
# Does It End?

*T* HIS clue has two parts: (1) How long does the romance last from start to finish? And (2) how long does it take you to get over it if it ends? Both parts are good indicators of whether it is love.

This is the only clue that can't be applied during the time the romance is in full swing. Naturally, you can't know how long it will last or how long it will take you to get over it if it hasn't stopped yet. This clue will nonetheless be of help to you as you look back on a past romance. It may ease your mind if you still have doubt about whether it was the real thing.

## Signs of Infatuation

If it is infatuation, *it stops the same way it starts—fast*. And for good reason. The few things you do like about the other person—even those strongly held at first—begin to wear thin. All those other things you don't have in common begin more and more to rear their ugly heads.

You begin to have quarrels, conflicts, even fights, and then doubts about your "love." Soon you break up.

The effects of an infatuation may not end all that fast. You may sigh over his or her picture a few weekends before you start to get over it. But you will, and before long you begin to smile to yourself and say, "What did I see in him (or her) anyway?" That was infatuation. And by and large an infatuation won't last long—*UNLESS*.

That "unless" is very, very important, so capitalize it, underline it, italicize it in your mind. We'll come back to it in just a moment. First, let's note the effect if it's real love.

## Signs of Love

If it's love, *it stops slowly.* It cannot do otherwise. If you have come to deeply love another person, it's going to take you more than a few weekends to get over it if it ends. Love involves meshing many, many facets of two personalities. You grow together and become a unit. In a very real sense, as the marriage vow states, the two really do become as one. The person becomes a basic part of you, of your own personality. If a break comes, you're just not going to be the same. In fact, you may never quite get over it for as long as you live.

Have you noticed what sometimes happens when two old people have loved each other for many, many years? They become so much a part of each other that they often act alike. They may even come to look a lot alike. And what happens if one of them dies and all those close ties are suddenly severed? In more than a few cases the other partner dies very soon, too. The one who died had become so much a part of the survivor's life that the survivor felt a deep loss and a longing to be reunited, even in death.

Young people can lose love too. Does that mean that if you've lost your beloved you cannot love again? A lot of people used to think that. They believed firmly that there was just one person created for each of us to marry, just as it was with Adam and Eve. I once knew a song called "I Want My Rib"—that is, the "one and only that is meant just for me."

We know now that this notion is false. Social scientists are certain that there are a number of persons in this world with whom each of us normally can have a genuine, deep-seated love that will last. There are, no doubt, several of these people within a short distance of your home base.

So if you've loved and lost, you have not been sentenced to being single the rest of your life. There is no such thing as a "one and only"—although after you're married it's a good plan not to keep looking over your shoulder at others. Once wed, just assume your mate is your one and only—for keeps.

## Infatuations Stop Fast—*Unless*

There is one major exception to the general rule that infatuations tend to break off early. An infatuation will end soon—*unless the couple becomes involved in mutually satisfying sexual relations*. If that happens, all bets are off on this clue. Sex will frustrate the usual test of time.

## Don't Cheat on the Test of Time

Usually, the longer a couple stays together and has a good relationship, the more certain they can be that it is real love. Why does this test not apply if they start to enjoy sex?

The answer is simple enough. *They may stay together just for the sex,* and not because they have all that much in common. That sex drive is so deep, so urgent. But its satisfaction does not last. In a few hours, or at most a few days, you are just as interested in sex as you were before. So the two people keep coming back to each other mainly for sex, not because they have lots of things in common and personalities that mesh. Thus they fool themselves into thinking they are well matched. They cheat on the test of time.

Studies indicate a good sexual relationship may hold a couple together as long as three to five years. But that's about it. Sex alone will not keep a couple together longer than that. So if they have no more in common than good sex, the relationship will wither away.

Good sex can fool you. A couple may think, "Well, the studies show that the longer a couple spends in courtship and engagement, the more likely it is that they've found real love. We've been going together three years now, so that must mean it's real love." Well, maybe so, maybe no. Three years together may mean that a relationship is good—but it may just mean that the sex life has been good.

Since sex is so deceptive, this is one of the most important reasons to resist having sex early in a relationship. You need to be very, very sure that the rest of your relationship is on sound ground before you muddy up your emotions with sex.

If you don't wait, you've robbed yourself of one of the best of all safeguards to keep you from acting rashly on an unsound relationship. Is it worth it to forfeit this kind of protection against future disaster, just for the sake of a few present thrills and joys? Quite apart from the moral and religious issues, or risks of STDs (Sexually Transmitted Diseases) or pregnancy, or disapproval by parents and society, this fact alone—this flunking the test of time—seems reason enough to hold off on sex until you marry. You need the test of time working for you, not against you. Those who cheat on the test of time cheat no one but themselves.

## "Making Up" the Test of Time

"But we're already involved in satisfying sex relations," one couple told me. "We think we love each other, but we want to be quite sure before we marry. Is there any way we can still apply the test of time to our relationship?"

A lot of couples face this problem. There is a way out for those who really want an answer, but the remedy is not easy. As in any experiment in science, the variable—in this case, sex—must be isolated. That is, the relationship of the couple must be observed and tested *apart from* the sexual factor. There are two ways to do this.

1. What the serious couple probably must do is arrange a rather lengthy separation, so they can't get at each other sexually. This must be for at least three or four months. They can stay in touch by mail, fax, and phone, but they must avoid all opportunities for sex. If their interest in each other survives the crisis of being apart that long, it's a pretty good sign that their interest involves love, not just sex alone.

2. "But," couples ask me, "why must we stay apart? Can't we just vow not to have sex for that same period of time, and go on seeing each other as usual?" No, not unless you have very strong willpower—or *won't* power! The reason is simple. Once a couple has established a habit of having sex, it is almost impossible for them to be alone together without doing it. One kiss leads to another and wham! They're back at it again. Like the

alcoholic who sneaks one drink, they may find that they just can't stop. So a conscious choice to get away from each other for a fairly long time is for most couples the only way. But by doing so they can lay claim once more to that crucial test of time.

The decision to stay apart must be the couple's own. If parents or others try to force such a separation, the couple may just set their brakes and vow to ride out the test period. Then they rush back into each other's arms. The separation test won't work unless the couple themselves want to make it work. It's a bitter pill, but it's the only sure cure—and well worth the swallowing.

Let's pause now and look more closely at the whole question of premarital sex.

# ... **10** .......

## To Be or
## Not to Be—
## A Virgin

W HETHER or not to save sex for marriage is still a big question for most young people. The average youth is torn between strong arguments for it and against it.

On the one hand, some segments of our society are dead set against you going all the way with sex unless you're married to your partner. This taboo is doubly strict in rural areas and if you're female.[1] If that strikes you as being unfair, you're quite right. But a double standard does exist, and no girl or woman can safely ignore that fact. Fair or not, the double standard will no doubt continue to exist until science finds some way for men to have babies. That may take a while! In addition to strong pressures against premarital sex laid down by society at large, the main religious bodies in America strictly oppose sex outside of marriage. Parents, too, are nearly unanimous in opposing premarital sex—again, especially for females.

All these factors and more—risks of pregnancy, Sexually Transmitted Diseases (STDs), etc. should provide cause for pause for any serious young person. It takes a mighty strong person to fly in the face of harsh social pressures and get away with it. It's not likely that you are one of those rather rare exceptions.

On the other hand, the sex drive for the normal young person may at times be powerful and hard to control. Lures toward sex may be extremely urgent. Even the most strong-willed person may on occasion be sorely tempted to go all the way.

Also, the modern young person's peer group is probably much more tolerant of premarital sex.[2] In the past, persons in one's own age group tended to show disapproval. That was an added nudge to hold the line. But today's youth are less quick to condemn premarital sex than their elders were. Many young people believe that what people do in their sex life is nobody's business but their own. That's not true, but some like to think it is.

Still other factors make it harder now for a young person to say no to premarital sex. Birth control devices are easy to obtain, and some are highly effective. If a couple "gets caught," it's easier to get an abortion (as of now). Most cases of STDs can now be cured. And most couples find it easy to be alone, with no adults around.

So if we add it all up, the picture seems clear. Sex is now a mighty tough urge to resist. The view of some young people seems to be, "Why fight it? Let's go for it."

## Isn't Everybody Doing It?

Not at all. Large numbers of single persons in the United States are virgins, though it is hard to know for sure just how many. Dozens of studies have been made, but their findings still differ quite a lot. Some show that the amount of premarital sex is no more now than before.

Others suggest a sharp increase. One survey of pregnant teens, 12–15 years of age, showed that the age at first intercourse ranged from 9–15 years, with a mean of 13.3 years.[3]

The group that years ago did the Kinsey study still doubts that there's been much change in U.S. sex habits in recent times. They claim the only sexual revolution in this country is what the mass media creates and promotes.[4] Some experts think Americans' sex behavior has not changed much in the last three generations and that youth today are just more open about it.

But most now think the rate of premarital sex has indeed increased.[5] The youth of today have long been much more tolerant of such behavior.[6] It should then come as no surprise that those permissive ideas are now being put into action. A change in attitude tends to bring changes in behavior.[7]

In fact, there are now many girls in junior high, and even some in fifth and sixth grade, who are getting pregnant. Children are having children!

Still, large numbers of youth and young adults are now questioning the wisdom of these trends, and they want some straight answers. "What do you think about having sex before marriage?" they ask. It's one of the most frequent questions put to teachers and counselors. It's a good one.

Yet what they *really* want to know is not so much *what* we think, but *why* we think it. Young people today are not much impressed by pious platitudes and mumbled morality. They demand honest answers based on proven facts. If premarital sex is not wise or is wrong, they have to know the reasons.

And why not? After all, what they do about sex will have to be their own decision. When they're in a bedroom or in the back seat of a car breathing hard, they are on their own. Mom and Dad and teachers and preachers can't help them then.

## Can the Trend Be Turned?

Yes, it can be, but it won't be easy. I think this is a great generation of young people. They are for the most part open and smart. I know. Each year I speak to about 50,000 of them in colleges, high school assemblies, and junior highs. I never preach at or moralize to them. I just give them solid facts backed up with sound research.

And they respond. In every case where they have done a before/after attitude survey, the results are the same. I never once say "do it" or "don't do it." Yet great numbers of the youth change their minds in the direction of rejecting sex before marriage. The changes are almost unbelievable.

At the Ft. Atkinson, Wisconsin, high school, 171 of their 600 students moved toward rejection; 110 of those moved from undecided to rejection.

Before the assembly at the Tomah, Wisconsin, public high, students favored sex before marriage by two to one. After that assembly, it was found that about 66% of their 800 students had changed their minds in the direction of repudiating it. Here are the results:

| Premarital Sex is: | Before Talk | After | % of Change |
|---|---|---|---|
| Very Wise | 11% | 2% | -9% |
| Wise | 29% | 6% | -23% |
| Undecided | 40% | 38% | -2% |
| Unwise | 12% | 45% | +33% |
| Very Unwise | 8% | 9% | + 1% |

Before the assembly, students favored premarital sex two to one; afterward they rejected it almost seven to one.[8]

Big shifts in thinking are also being produced in the junior highs and middle schools when I speak.

If we just present the facts right, these young people will respond in amazing numbers. All we have to do is get to more and more of them with this same kind of message.* Churches as well as schools must move to meet this challenge. Search Institute has now found that mainline Protestant churches lose many of their youth at about high school age. Why did these adolescents drop away? Half of those who still stayed in church expressed "strong interest" in getting help with their questions about sexuality.[9] And I find large numbers of students in Catholic high schools are also already having sex. More and more churches—Catholic and Protestant—are deeply concerned about this problem. Hence much of my speaking now is to youth *and* parents together in local churches.

## The Arguments, Pro and Con

Over the years, the subject of sex before marriage came up in each college class I taught on marriage and the family. I'd turn the question right back to the students. I would draw a line down the middle of the blackboard. "OK, now you tell me whether premarital sex is smart or not. Give me all the arguments both for and against it that you've ever heard." Then I'd list all the arguments on the board in two columns. When they were all there in front of us, we'd discuss each of them. If there were research studies that might apply to any point, pro or con, I laid those facts before the group. "Now make up your own mind," I would say.

---

*To schedule Dr. Short for speaking, write to: 505 So. Miller Ave., Lafayette, CO 80026, or phone 303-666-5025.

A full list of arguments for and against premarital sex appears on pages 98-101. Groups of college and high school students over the past 25 years contributed to the list. I edited it just enough to weed out duplicate or out-of-date items.

The purpose of the list is to help you decide whether premarital sex makes sense. So mark your own answers and judge for yourself. How wise or unwise do you think it is? Be honest—and consistent.

After you've marked your checklist, we can consider what scientific studies have found. How does premarital sex affect your chances for a good marriage? Is sex before marriage a plus or a minus? Some of the findings may surprise you.

## Eleven Known Facts

Science has established eleven facts concerning the probable effect of premarital sex on your marriage.

Fact 1. *Premarital sex tends to break up couples.* Other things being equal, couples who engage in sex are more likely to break up before marriage than those who do not.[10] So what about the young woman who gives in to sex in the hope that she won't lose her young man? ("I'm afraid if I don't give in, he'll cut out.") She would more likely *hold him* if she *holds out*. And if he does cut out— good riddance! If sex is all he wants, you are better off without him.

Fact 2. *Many men and women do not want to marry a person who has had intercourse with someone else.* Some fellows do their level best to reduce the number of virgins in the population! Yet when it comes time to marry, they don't want a girl who's been pawed over by other guys. Their strange logic seems to be: "It's OK for me to have sex with the girl you marry, but it's not OK for you to have sex with mine."

# CHECKLIST OF ARGUMENTS FOR AND AGAINST PREMARITAL SEXUAL INTERCOURSE*

A. Arguments offered for: Indicate for each item the degree of soundness or unsoundness, in your judgment, of that argument for premarital intercourse.

|  | Very sound | Fairly sound | Unde-cided | Fairly unsound | Very unsound |
|---|---|---|---|---|---|
| 1. It is the highest expression of human love. | | | | | |
| 2. It is the natural expression of sex. | | | | | |
| 3. It avoids frustrations aroused by petting. | | | | | |
| 4. It is a maturing experience. | | | | | |
| 5. A student cannot afford marriage. | | | | | |
| 6. It is a way a student can rebel if parents will not allow marriage. | | | | | |
| 7. It is a way to rebel against society. | | | | | |
| 8. It avoids responsibilities of marriage. | | | | | |
| 9. It is a method of getting a mate. | | | | | |
| 10. It brings pleasure, enjoyment, fulfillment. | | | | | |
| 11. It seems increasingly more socially acceptable. | | | | | |
| 12. It is condoned by other modern cultures. | | | | | |
| 13. It satisfies curiosity. | | | | | |
| 14. It is a test of physical compatibility. | | | | | |
| 15. It is a test of mental compatibility. | | | | | |
| 16. It fills a need for affection (loneliness). | | | | | |

*Persons who might wish to use this checklist to measure the thinking of members of a group should use some code to protect the identity of each member. Otherwise the results may not be accurate. Then have the group discuss each item

17. Why wait; the world may blow up tomorrow.
18. It's OK if you don't get discovered.
19. It can be used as an escape mechanism.
20. Some people have had experience living in a culture where premarital coitus was acceptable.
21. It is OK if done for fear of losing your desired mate.
22. Prohibitions inhibit expression of real love.
23. It is OK if the couple is engaged, planning marriage.
24. It is OK if they consider themselves married already.
25. Sexually experienced persons adjust more quickly to sex in marriage.
26. _____
27. _____

                                                    TOTALS

B. Arguments offered against: Indicate for each item the degree of soundness or unsoundness, in your judgment, of that argument against premarital intercourse.

| | Very sound | Fairly sound | Unde-cided | Fairly unsound | Very unsound |
|---|---|---|---|---|---|
| 1. The fear and danger of pregnancy. | | | | | |
| 2. The danger of STDs and AIDS. | | | | | |
| 3. It causes guilt feelings. | | | | | |
| 4. It brings social disapproval, pressure, penalties. | | | | | |
| 5. The fear of being discovered. | | | | | |
| 6. It violates religious beliefs. | | | | | |

7. A stigma is on the unwed mother and child.

8. Pregnancy is especially a problem if one is unable to accept marriage responsibilities.

9. May be forced to marry before it is wise.

10. It interrupts normal life patterns (education, life plans, etc.).

11. It's a threat to the family as an institution.

12. Tends to prolong unsound relationships (infatuation) which normally would die except for sexual stimulation.

13. May lead to mental conflicts; in extreme cases, even mental illness or suicide.

14. Not likely to be as thrilling as anticipated due to abnormal conditions, fears, guilts.

15. Violates the ideal of chastity before marriage.

16. If you love your partner, you won't wish to expose him or her to probable negative consequences.

17. Abortions are dangerous, immoral, traumatic, maybe illegal.

18. It tends to lead to crime or prostitution.

19. It tends to break up the couple before marriage.

20. It leads to jealousy and doubts that your partner can be trusted.

21. It may lead to a pattern of fear, guilt connected with the sex act, even lasting into marriage.

22. It may impair the aesthetic (beautiful) aspect of sex in marriage.

23. Poor conditions for coitus usually prevail.
24. It tends to spoil relationships if pregnancy results.
25. If a child comes, it will likely be unwanted, and children *need* to be wanted.
26. Tends to lead to extramarital relations.
27. Causes loss of respect for self and sex partner.
28. Cheapens procreation, which is a sacred trust.
29. Many persons don't want to marry someone who has had intercourse with others.
30. Immaturity is reinforced—person wants the joy, pleasure of sex without any responsibilities.
31. The relationship may be exploitive, selfish.
32. Sexually experienced persons have less happy marriages.
33. Sexually experienced persons are more likely to divorce.
34. Sexually experienced persons are less happy with their married sex life.
35. _____
36. _____

TOTALS

Your Answer: In view of the above arguments both for and against, do *you* think sexual intercourse before marriage is (Check one):

____Very Wise    ____Wise    ____Undecided    ____Unwise    ____Very Unwise

In one Kinsey study, over half the college-level males under age 25 expected to marry a virgin, or at least a woman who had had sex with no one else.[11] That proportion may since have changed, but many women as well as men still secretly hold that hope. In fact, in a more recent survey of young men chosen for listing in *Who's Who among High School Students*, almost two out of three (63%) said they prefer to marry a virgin.

Fear of AIDS is another factor now.* A study published in 1988 showed that "Over half of the sexually active [college] students claim they have altered their behavior in some way as a result of this concern. And 15% of the nonactive students report that their concern has prevented them from becoming sexually active."[12]

Nor are men the only ones who prefer to marry a virgin. In fact, for both sexes, the more sexual experience the other person has had, the less desirable that person is. This is true not only for the choice of mates, but also for dates. And it applies to those who have had oral sex or same-sex experience as well. Both sexes prefer partners who have done no more than moderate petting—breast, or at most, genital fondling.[13]

Fact 3. *Those who have premarital sex tend to have less happy marriages.* On the whole, your chances of being happily married are better if you wait till you're wed to have sex. And the more premarital sex you have, the less likely you'll be happy in your marriage.[14]

Fact 4. *Those who have premarital sex are more likely to have their marriage end in divorce.* This follows from Fact 3. If a couple is unhappy with their marriage, they're more likely to get a divorce. And again, the more premarital sex the individuals have had, the greater the

---

*See the Appendix for more information on AIDS.

chance of divorce.[15] It seems to make good sense to choose a one and only, " 'til death do us part."

Fact 5. *Persons and couples who have had premarital sex are more likely to have extramarital affairs as well.* That is especially true of females. The Kinsey report showed that women who had sex before marriage were *more than twice* as likely to cheat on their husbands as women who were virgins at the time of their marriage. The same is true of men. The more premarital sex a person has had, the more likely he or she is to commit adultery.[16]

This should come as no surprise. Take these cases. Suppose after marriage one meets a person one used to date. He meets the gal on a business trip. Or she has lunch with the guy. It could be all very innocent. But if the couple has had sex with each other before, are they more likely or less likely to end up in bed together than if they had never ever had sex with each other before? I'll give you three guesses and the first two don't count!

Of course, once a couple have had sex with each other, it is much, much easier to do the same thing again, married or not. This factor may well be the most serious consequence of all for a marriage. Few wives, and even fewer husbands, are able to tolerate—much less approve—acts of adultery on the part of their spouse. Even in cases where it never gets discovered by the spouse, adultery may well drive a deep wedge between the couple. Suspicions do creep in.

Fact 6. *Having premarital sex may fool you into marrying a person who is not right for you.* As we have seen, sex can blind you. You may believe you've found real love, when in fact it is only sex that has held you together. If you wait for sex until you're quite sure you have a sound relationship *without* sex, you can avoid this tragic error. Once your relationship is firmly established, then your married sex life becomes a beautiful, wondrous bonus. It will tie you together even more completely in your marriage.

The next two facts are best taken together. The first is a short-term plus, but the second a long-range minus.

Fact 7. *Persons and couples with premarital sex experience tend to achieve sexual satisfaction sooner after they are married. However . . .*

Fact 8. *They are likely to be less satisfied overall with their sex life during marriage.* That is, they adjust to sex more quickly, but their overall adjustment is less satisfying than it is with couples who wait for sex until after they wed.

Learning to have good sex is in part a physical skill. In that sense it is like learning to play the piano or to ride a bicycle. You don't just sit down to the keyboard and rattle off a sonata by Mozart. Nor do you hop on a bike for the first time and sail off down the road. At first you make some mistakes. You fall over. You skin shins. You have to learn just when to turn the wheel so you won't fall over on your face. The more you practice any motor skill, the better you get at it.

Thus, married or not, your first sexual experience is not likely to be all that great, especially if you're female. Both of you are bound to be a bit clumsy. It will take time for virgin newlyweds to get their sex life in order, no matter how much they love each other. But once they get the hang of it, their sex life tends to be happier than that of those who have experienced sex before marriage.

Why should sexually experienced persons be less satisfied with their married sex life? One reason is that their premarital sex experience can rise to haunt them. Suppose that a certain wife has an orgasm about half the time when she and her husband have intercourse. She never has more than one climax during coitus. She is, in fact, well above the national average, since only 30% of U.S. women orgasm each time there is penetration.[17]

But what if the man she marries has had sex with other partners before? Isn't he likely to compare his wife's sexual "performance" with that of his previous partners? And so will the wife if she has had sex with other men. They can scarcely avoid that.

Now, people differ widely in their sexual nature and skills. Some are highly active, some are more reserved. What if in the past this man had sex with a woman who had several "whoopee boi-oi-oing" orgasms each time they had intercourse? This is not too common, but it does happen. Will his memories of such experiences help or hinder his adjustment to sex with his wife? Will he be satisfied with his wife's more reserved response? Remember, her responses are well above average, yet he may feel cheated and unhappy because of the comparison.

Now suppose that this same woman is married to a man who, like herself, has had sex with no one else. The only sex they have known is with each other. Are they not much more likely to be fully satisfied with the sex life they share? What they have is good, so they're happy with it. The statistics are clearly on their side.

"But Prof," you may say. "They are more satisfied out of ignorance." So what! If they want to have a happy sex life (and who of us does not?) and being a virgin at marriage is the best way to get it, who is to say them nay?

## Married Sex Is Best

Almost any wife and husband can work out a happy sexual adjustment if they love each other. Any loving couple's sex life is likely to be just fine. When they have a warm, compatible relationship, they can with very few exceptions work out a good sex life. A *Redbook* magazine poll of tens of thousands of married men and women revealed that the vast majority are satisfied with their sex life together.[18] Sex in the context of a meaningful, lasting relationship is by far the best sex. If you've never had sex with someone you truly love, you just don't know what good sex is all about! Sex at only the physical level scarcely scratches the surface of deep meaning and true satisfaction. In fact, it's hardly even human. After all, any old dog or hog can perform pure sex! The purely physical concept of sex is quite beneath us as human persons. It's not worthy of our best selves.[19]

## Total Sex

No matter how skilled and exotic and explosive a merely physical sexual experience may be, it cannot begin to match total sex. Total sex involves the completion and conjoining of total personalities. It merges the minds, the emotions, and the social and spiritual selves of a couple, as well as their two bodies. The two truly do become one. They can actually be worshiping God in the act of having sex. No sensible person should want to settle for anything less than that kind of sex.

Author Bill (*My Shadow Ran Fast*)[20] Sands is an ex-con who made good. He once hammered home this point about total sex to students at the University of Wisconsin–Platteville. Some of the students were stunned by his words.

A young man asked Sands what he thought about having sex with others besides his wife. He replied, "I see no point in it. Why should I settle for hamburger when I can have steak?"

It seems he had found a truly fine love, and with it a fine sex life. He was right. There's more to good sex than a breathless bounce in bed!

## If You're Engaged—Why Wait?

Couples who have avoided sex while dating are more likely to become sexually active once they're engaged. "After all," they reason, "we fully intend to marry. We're already publicly committed to each other, even if it's not yet in writing. If we take care to avoid being discovered and if we avert pregnancy, why wait?"

On the face of it, the arguments sound convincing. But what if you do get discovered? What if the woman does get pregnant? And what if you break up? One out of every three engagements in the United States is broken, and premarital sex is in itself one big causal factor.

Smart couples will not fail to consider these facts. But even if none of these things happen, there is one other grave danger that is overlooked far too often.

Premarital sexual experience may actually deprive you of much of the sexual joy you can and should have after you marry. By rushing into the joys of premarital sex, you may rob yourself of the deeper, more permanent, joys of total sex. Fact 9 explains how and why this can occur. Unlike most of the facts we have discussed, this one applies as much or more severely to those who have had sex with no one other than the one they wed.

Fact 9. *Poor premarital sexual habits can be carried over to spoil sex in marriage*. Sadly enough, this happens a lot. The Kinsey studies found that more than half of American wives are in some degree either not willing or not able to share sex freely and fully with their husbands. They have guilts and fears. They are hesitant or inhibited.

It's been a long time since the Kinsey research, and we hope this high rate is lower now. Still, many wives—and to a lesser extent their husbands—have poor attitudes about sex even now, according to the Hite reports.[21]

Why is this so? A number of reasons are often cited. Some in our society still cling to some early Victorian prudery about sex. Then, too, many Christians have adopted St. Paul's view that sex is "of the flesh" and hence to be shunned. They believe it is at best something that is not quite nice. Then there has no doubt been poor sex education in home, church, and school. And unhealthy attitudes have been handed down by our elders. In all, Americans do have lots of "hang-up hangovers" from the past.

But in addition to these more familiar reasons for lack of sexual enjoyment, there is a factor that has escaped the attention it deserves. What is this culprit? It is *premarital intercourse*, along with other guilt-producing premarital sex acts.

## Sexual Salivation

This is my term for that process by which premarital sex often spoils sex in marriage. Why? The term is suggested by that famous experiment of the Russian scientist Pavlov, and his pooch. Like any normal dog, when it saw food, the dog salivated—its mouth would water. Each time the dog was shown food, Pavlov rang a bell. Soon the dog was trained (or conditioned) to salivate any time the bell rang, even when no food was in sight. The real *cause* of salivation—the food—was gone, yet when the bell was rung, the dog went right on salivating anyway.

So it is with premarital sex. Many sexual "hang-ups" in marriage have their roots in a similar process. Here's how "sexual salivation" works.

Since premarital sex is still a social and religious no-no, illicit sex acts usually produce some degree of guilt, fear, and loss of self-esteem. This can apply to both partners, but it is especially true for women. They feel guilt, since they are doing what they feel they should not do. They lose self-respect, since they are not living up to their own ideals. And they are afraid of three things: getting caught in the act of sex, getting pregnant, and perhaps contracting an STD.

So what may happen if you get into a pattern of premarital sex? Whether you're engaged or not, each time you have sex, you "salivate"—you feel guilt and fear and loss of self-respect. Over and over again this happens. You have sex, you feel fear and guilt and remorse. In time, all of these negative feelings become associated with the sex act itself. As the dog came to associate food with the bell, you learn to tie sex with unhealthy feelings.

Now suppose you do get married. Once wed, you have no further need to feel guilt, fear, and remorse when you engage in sex. Once you have that piece of paper, you have social license to have just about any kind of sex you choose. So as soon as the ceremony is over, you will suddenly be able to forget all about the past—right? You can fall into your spouse's arms on the honeymoon and be utterly uninhibited—right? You will shed all that backlog of guilt, fear, and shame like a snake sheds its skin in summer—right?

*Wrong!* To the extent you learned to associate sex with guilt and fear and shame *before* the wedding, you will in some measure feel that way *afterward.*

Just as with the dog's food, the causes of the response have been removed. Still, every time you two "ring the bell" by having sex, that guilt and fear and shame will come back to haunt you. It may take months or even years for you to recondition yourselves. Only then can your sex life be full and free.

Small wonder so many husbands and wives are inhibited.

Consider the case of Jim and Mary. They have been happily married for many years. Mary had sex with no one but Jim before they married, but they did have sex with each other for about 18 months before the wedding. They were lucky. They got by without a pregnancy, and they were never caught in the act of sex.

Did that mean they were home free? Hardly. Sexual salivation caught up with them. After ten years and four children, Mary was still in some measure unable to give herself fully and freely in sex to her husband. Sad indeed.

Were Jim and Mary just a couple of dummies? Not at all. They both had college degrees in sociology. Both became successful social workers. They had reliable information about sex and were alert to new insights in the field of married love.

But they also had a deep interest in religion. It was highly important to them to behave in ways they felt were right. So even though they got by without being discovered or without a premarital pregnancy, sexual salivation took a heavy toll. The price they paid was a dear one—the loss of a full, free sex experience through their early years of marriage. Is premarital sex really worth all that?

## Illicit Sex as Forbidden Fruit

The sexual salivation process before marriage may in part be responsible for extramarital sex—adultery—in later life. Indulging in "forbidden fruit" brings special pleasure and excitement. The watermelon swiped from the farmer's patch may taste far better than the one you buy from him.

Premarital sex is considered illicit, wrong, especially by most religious folk. It is forbidden fruit—which may bring that special pleasure and excitement.

After marriage, sex is no longer forbidden. Couples accustomed to the excitement of forbidden fruit may find married sex to be a bit dull. Might this tempt a spouse to try to find greater excitement outside the marriage bond—which is another kind of forbidden fruit?

Fact 10. *Guilt may push a couple into a bad marriage.* Many persons (especially those with a deep religious faith or background) will feel that they should have sex only with the person they wed and no one else. So they may feel duty-bound to marry a person they have had sex with. As a result, this guilt and sense of obligation may push them into a poor marriage.

For instance, let's assume that a couple feel certain that they are in love. They get engaged. "Since we will soon marry anyway," they reason, "we'll just fudge a bit and start having sex." (A risky plan, remember, since one of every three engaged couples breaks up without marrying.) But later one or both develop some doubts. "Maybe this isn't love after all. Maybe we ought to break up." That would be the smart thing to do. But since they have already shared the sex, they feel obliged to go ahead with the wedding anyway—with tragic results.

It happens a lot more often than most people think.

Fact 11. *Premarital sex robs a couple of "sexual cement."* The sex act is the most intimate of all human behaviors. If done with love, it bonds a couple together in a unique way. It is so wonderful that it keeps them coming back to each other even though there may be real problems— like money, in-laws, etc.—to be worked out in their relationship.

I call this bonding "sexual cement," since it is so strong that it can hold a couple together for up to three to five years. Here's why it is of vital importance to hold off having sex until after you're wed so it can help you make your marriage work out.

This is how it works.

Two things we know. First, *the roughest period of adjustment for a couple in their marriage is the first five years.* That's when most divorces occur. The curve looks like this:

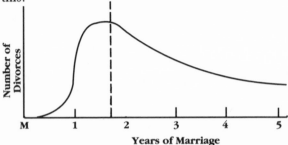

**Years of Marriage**

The peak problem years are the very first three. Now let's look at the second thing we know.

*The peak of sexual excitement and thrill of having intercourse occurs in most cases in the very first year* that a couple starts to have sex with each other. That curve looks like this:

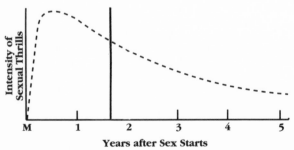

**Years after Sex Starts**

The very peak of their sexual thrills will likely occur in the very first year, followed by a gradual decline. After five years it has tended to level out so that sex becomes only one of many very important things to hold the couple together.

Now let's do some comparing. Suppose the couple begin having sex two years before they marry. Putting one curve over the other, we get:

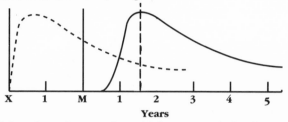

Right when the couple need it most to help them over the very roughest years of adjustment in their marriage, much of that wonderful sexual cement has already been spent.

How sad! One of the most powerful bonding forces available to any newlyweds has already lost a large portion of its thrilling appeal. That precious bonding of sex that could have helped hold them together while they worked out their problems has been largely lost.

But what if the couple do wait until marriage to have their first sexual intercourse? Again putting the two curves together, we get:

Right when they need it most, they have those wondrous first years of their sex life to keep them coming back together until they can work out their problems and save their marriage. What a wonderful asset sex can be!

## Whether—Plus How Much and with Whom

Now let's sum up the 11 known facts about sex before marriage. Other things being equal, if you have premarital sex you are more likely to:

1. Break up before you marry.
2. Scare off anyone who wants to marry a virgin.
3. Be less happy in your marriage.
4. Get a divorce.
5. Commit adultery after you marry.
6. Be fooled into marrying for the wrong reasons.
7. Achieve married sex happiness quicker, *but*
8. Be less satisfied with your married sex life.
9. Spoil total sex due to sexual salivation.
10. Have guilt feelings that may nudge you into a poor marriage.
11. Be deprived of that all-important "sexual cement" right when you need it the most.

That's a pretty impressive list!

It is not only significant *whether* you have premarital sex, but also *how much* you have. The more of it you have, the greater the impact of the 11 facts on your marriage.

It also matters *with whom* you have premarital sex. If you have sex only with the person you marry, Facts 1, 9 and 11 still apply to you, but for the most part the other seven facts apply less harshly than if you have sex with other persons as well.

## But Why Not Try Out Sex?

Some believe they need to test out sex before marriage. Since good sex adjustment is important, they want to know beforehand what that part of their relationship will be like. "You wouldn't buy a used car without first trying it out," a guy may say. "So why marry without trying out sex?"

On its face, that argument may sound logical—although it isn't very flattering to a woman to compare her to a used car! Like *Playboy* magazine, the guy seems to see a girl as a "plaything." She is a commodity to be acquired and used, not a life partner to be loved and cherished. That may be fine if he's shopping only for a sex object, but if he's looking for a life mate, it leaves much to be desired.

So a lot depends on what the "sex shopper" has in mind. Does he seriously intend to sign a contract, or is he looking just for the fun of it? A smart car salesman quickly spots the "joy ride only" customer. Once he does, he's not likely to allow that person any more trial runs with his fleet. The smart young woman will do the same with the man who wants to "try her out" in bed. There are several reasons the "try it out first" idea won't hold water—even in a waterbed!

## The Teacher and the Plumber

Some people make one very big mistake. They assume that sex outside of marriage is going to be a valid sample of what sex will be like within marriage. But premarital sex is not a true test. Consider this case history.

A teacher in her late twenties and a young plumber became close friends. They had a great deal in common. The more time they spent with each other, the more certain they were that their love was real.

But they had one big problem. He said he would not agree to marry her unless they first tested out their sexual adjustment. To this she simply could not agree. She felt strongly that sex is only for marriage. To try it out beforehand, even with one she loved, went against her every belief and feeling. Yet he persisted. He just refused to marry her otherwise. Finally, with great reluctance and deep feelings of guilt and fear, she agreed to submit to sex rather than lose her beloved.

Any good marriage counselor could guess how that experiment would turn out. The teacher's nervous fears and guilts made her so anxious and worried that the sex session was a dismal failure. Convinced that their sex life would never work out, the plumber broke off the engagement, leaving his girlfriend in a state of shock and deep depression. Not only had she lost her virginity; she had also lost her man.

But they did have a lot in common, so after a while they drifted back together. Again they talked of marriage. He suggested that maybe one try-out of sex was not enough, and perhaps they should try it again! Despite grave misgivings, she finally gave in. But in view of the previous failure, she was even more anxious and tense. He decided that it just wasn't going to work. He cut out for good, and she ended up in a psychiatrist's office.

How foolish for the man to assume from one or two premarital experiments that their whole married sex life would not be good! In the first place, the first sexual experience of any woman is not likely to be all that good—married or not. But if her first sex comes *after* she's married, the chances for success are far better. Once wed, she need feel no guilt, no fear, no remorse. She can relax and release herself to sex much more fully and freely. Premarital sex doesn't really give sex a fair trial. Indeed, it may even spoil good sex in marriage.

## It's Not Necessary to Try Sex First

If you have real love going for you, don't worry about your sex life being good. It will be. The exceptions to that rule are so rare that you can safely ignore the issue. If you truly love and respect your spouse, just relax. You will no doubt be able to work things out in your sex life. If that does not happen quite as soon as you think it should, read some good books or get some counseling to help you out. *Mutual love and tender caring are far more important in sexual adjustment than are smooth techniques and wildly erotic responses.* Above all, be relaxed and honest and considerate of each other. Nature will take care of the rest.

*Sex Is Never an Emergency*—that's the title of a book.[22] It suggests an essential point that's often overlooked. Sex is the only major human drive that does not have to be satisfied. You can't survive without eating and drinking, but the sex drive can be denied indefinitely. As sex therapist L. G. Baker put it, "Clearly the sex drive is not the same, as say, the hunger drive. . . . Nobody ever dies for want of sexual nutrients! . . ." Sex is not a necessity. "We tend to confuse the ability to do 'it' with the *need* to. . . . good sex never saved a bad marriage"[23]—or, I might add, never made a good one, either.

Sex may be important, but it's not crucial to the good life. A person can go a full lifetime without sex and suffer no serious damage. Priests, nuns, and other celibates have been proving that for centuries.

Girls report that some boys try to mislead them on this point. During an especially torrid "breathing hard" session, the boy may get highly aroused. Then his argument goes something like this: "Oh, Suzy, I'm too excited to stop. We've gone this far, you just have to let me go all the way. I'll just die if you don't let me. I've just gotta!" Well, he doesn't "just gotta!" If he doesn't get to have intercourse right then, he's not going to break out in purple pimples! He won't suffer any permanent brain damage—or body damage either. It won't even stunt the poor boy's growth. He may have to run around the block a time or two before he goes home, but he can do that.

Then the next time those two had better call a halt to things before he gets so fired up. Some guys try to use force when they get that excited. That can lead to some pretty tense moments, and maybe lots of regrets—even date rape.[24] Any time anyone does anything sexual to you against your will, that is a crime. Furthermore, in most states, any male who has intercourse with an underage female is guilty of statutory rape, even if she consents.

## What Every Girl Needs to Know

Girls are more likely than boys to be confused by these strong sexual feelings. Partly because of our society's double standard, there is a basic difference in what sex means to males and what it means to females. A man may want sex with just about anything that wears a skirt. He can enjoy sex with a pick-up or a prostitute, even though he feels no affection for her at all. But most women in our culture won't have sex with just any guy who happens to come along. For them, love and sex should go together. The typical woman won't agree to sex unless she believes she loves the man.

Unless a woman knows about this basic difference between females and males, she may be in for trouble. Say she goes out with a man she's very fond of. They park in a lonely spot. He comes on real strong with the sex bit. He seems to have international forelimbs—Russian hands and Roman fingers! His advances grow more and more urgent. She doesn't have to read a book to find out what's on his mind. He wants to have sex with her. Should she let him or not?

If she doesn't know the facts of life about guys, she may wrongly reason something like this: "I wouldn't want to have sex with a guy unless I loved him. Johnny clearly wants to have sex with me. That must mean he loves me."

Don't you believe it, Suzy! He may just be looking for a handy solution to his present problem. He might have just as much interest in any female who happens to be within reach. The idea of love may never have entered his hot little mind.

## The Tenderness Trap

This situation can get even more complex. Suppose Johnny has been around enough to know all about this particular difference between females and males. He knows full well that women seldom agree to sex unless they think there is real love in the relationship. So what does Mr. Bright Boy do? You guessed it. If all else fails, he may resort to wild and ardent claims of undying love for her.

Now if she's smart, Suzy will be wary. She'd best not believe his claims of love unless his attitudes and actions support his words. She should ask herself: "Has he over a long period of time fully proven that he really does love me? Has he been kind and considerate? Does he want what's good for me as well as for himself? Is he willing to put me at great risk just to get his own pleasure?" He's saying, "I love you very much," but maybe what he really means is, "I sure would like to score with you."

We hasten to say that many males have very high principles and would not be guilty of such deceit. But better for a woman to be safe than sorry.

# Keeping Sex in Its Proper Place

$D$ o you hope some day to have a happy and lasting marriage? If so, you may want to "play the odds" by steering clear of premarital sex. As the "eleven known facts" just discussed would suggest, your chances for a good marriage seem far better if you wait for the wedding.

Yet your sex urge is still there. It won't "just go away"— and you don't want it to. You want to find some healthy way to cope with it. How can you stay sensitive to the sex urge, yet avoid messing up or going all the way? Where is it smart to stop? How far is too far?

## From Full Repression to Full Expression

The many stages of sexual arousal form a spectrum ranging from one extreme to the other.[1] One extreme is full repression, complete denial of the sex urge. The other extreme is going all the way to intercourse. Starting with repression, each stage brings deeper sexual excitement.

## The road to arousal

| | Necking | | | | Light petting | | | Heavy petting | | | | |
|---|---|---|---|---|---|---|---|---|---|---|---|---|
| **FULL REPRESSION** | Holding hands | Hugging | Casual kissing | Serious kissing | French kissing (?) | Breasts covered | Breasts bared | Genitals covered | Genitals bared | Oral sex (?) | Genital to genital | **SEXUAL INTERCOURSE** |

Two of the stages are hard to place on the chart. French or deep kissing (what I call tongue-in-cheek kissing!) is by strict definition a last stage of necking. But its arousing effect on some may be so intense it could be classed as petting. Then again it may turn some people off completely. (Good grief—all those germs!) In like manner oral sex—mouth to genital—will likely have a negative effect on many people, especially women. (Yuck! I don't want my mouth *there!*) It is largely a male invention anyway.

So how far should you go down the road to arousal? And once you've set a limit on how far to go, how can you hold the line? You must find the right answers for yourself, but here are five general principles which may help you decide what is best for you.

Principle 1. *Avoid the two extremes.* We have seen why it is hazardous to go all the way before marriage. The long-term risks hardly seem worth the sensual thrills of the moment.

But it is equally dangerous to take the opposite extreme and fully repress the sex urge. If you try to keep the lid on it by refusing to admit it's there, you're failing to deal with it wisely.

A repressed desire does not die. It just gets pushed out of the conscious mind and into the subconscious, where it smolders and festers, waiting its chance to be expressed in some hidden form. If you don't deal with it directly and consciously, it lurks in the shadows. It gets distorted and dangerous. Note this example from the past.

Jane was utterly ignorant about sex when she married John. In fact, when John kissed her once on a date she thought he had made her pregnant! (Hard to believe that she could think that, but she did!) During more than 25 years of marriage she saw sex as repulsive and dirty. She resisted all of John's normal advances. Several times she even tried to get doctors to prescribe that she should never have sex again.

Finally, as she approached menopause, I gave her a book aimed mainly at helping the inhibited wife.[2] Later, as she returned it, tears streamed down her cheeks. "Oh, if only I'd read this book 30 years ago," she sobbed. "It would have saved me a lifetime of hell!" She had so repressed her sexuality that she and her husband were robbed of the normal joys of sharing their married love through sex.

In extreme cases, the sex urge may be denied (suppressed) so fully that it is in great measure destroyed. One law of biology is: Use it or lose it. Fish that live in caves with no light lose their sight. An arm that's never used will atrophy. A person confined to bed for many months must learn to walk all over again.

So it is with the sex urge. It is a fine and precious gift when used in the right way, but a potential source of tragedy when it is not. It would seem wise for young people to give the sex urge enough expression to keep it warm and alive for marriage, while avoiding the dangers of its misuse.

It is hard to say which extreme holds the harsher hazards—total expression or total repression or suppression of the sex urge. Both can ruin lives. That's why Principle 1 is: Avoid both extremes.

Principle 2. *Don't light more fires than you put out.* If your goal is avoiding the two extremes—full repression and full expression—the trick is to give the sex drive a healthy expression without going too far. But how far is far enough?

The answer to that question may depend on your age and maturity, your level of willpower, your ability to keep control of yourself, and your situation at a given time. Can you say no to yourself and others—and mean it?

Deciding how far to go will also depend on how well you know and like the other person. How long have you been seeing a lot of each other? How much can you trust the other person—and yourself? Are you willing to accept full responsibility for everything you do?

No one rule of thumb will apply in every case to every person. We are all different. Some may find that they must stop at necking. Others may find they can go farther with no real problems. You must determine for yourself how far down the road to arousal you can safely go.

But one principle would seem sound for all to follow. Express your warm emotions enough to keep them alive and healthy, but don't go so far that you're in even worse emotional shape when you stop than you were before. Don't arouse more passion than you satisfy, or you'll end up restless and frustrated and full of gnawing desire. If you're more disturbed and unhappy than you were to begin with, just what have you gained? Besides, you're probably skating on thin ice. Next time you may not be able to stop.

Principle 3. *Avoid all chance of pregnancy.* This may strike you as strange. If you're not going to have inter-course, why worry about pregnancy?

A virgin can conceive. It doesn't happen often, but it's possible. Some doctors report that they come upon 3 to 4 cases every year. The social services director in a small Illinois town told me after my program there: "I'm so glad you warned these young people that they can get a pregnancy without ever having intercourse. We are now getting about one such case a year right in this small town." These women had never had penetration yet were pregnant.

How can that be? For a woman to get pregnant, a sperm must fertilize an ovum. So how can a sperm reach the egg without intercourse? Very simple. It enters from the outside.

A sperm has a head—to fertilize the ovum—and a tail. What's the tail for? Lo-comotion—just like a tad-pole.

**Sperm**

And sperm can swim around in any favorably moist substance that's at body temperature. What is more, there are millions of them in every male ejaculation or sexual discharge. Estimates of the number of live sperm in each discharge range all the way from two million up to 500 million. Now that's a whale of a lot of little sperm—and every one of them has one sole goal: Get the egg! Get the egg!

If a couple engages in heavy petting and the male ejaculates, some of the discharge may be introduced to the moist surface of the female genitals—the vulva—via the fingers, or in genital-to-genital petting. If they've been petting heavily, her genitals—inside and out—are pretty sure to be moist and at body heat. An excellent environment for sperm swimming!

Yes, you guessed it. Hundreds of live sperm may find their way right in through the opening of the vagina. Even if she has a hymen, there has to be some opening there or she couldn't menstruate. The sperm wriggle their way up in the vagina, in through the cervix and uterus, into the fallopian tubes, and wham! Another virgin has conceived.

Hence, to avoid all chance of pregnancy, you must at the very least set your limit short of genital-to-genital petting. If you do pet until the male reaches climax, you must take care that none of the ejaculate is introduced to the vulva or vagina.

## A Tale of Two Females

But is it all that bad for a young woman to get pregnant outside of marriage? Consider the responses of two young women who came to my office.

One young woman comes in with her husband. Both have had my course in marriage and they've come back to share some pleasant moments with "Prof." It's clear from the time they enter the room that they can hardly wait to break their news. "Prof, you'll never guess what's going to happen to us in August," she finally says—just as if nobody's ever had a baby before. They clasp hands, beaming. They are utterly delighted and proud that she is growing their very own baby in her womb. It is a joyous occasion for all concerned.

Now contrast that scene with a visit from an unwed female student. As she comes through the door, there's a dark cloud of gloom hanging over her head. "My God, Prof," she blurts out through sobs. "I'm going to have a baby! What am I going to do?" She clearly hates the fact that she's growing another little human being in her body. She's bitter and depressed and confused. Suicide has crossed her mind. She'd give anything in the world if she were not pregnant. What a contrast to the utter happiness of the married couple!

Well, what can this young woman do? There's no really good answer. But let's consider her options.

If the father is mature and responsible and if they love each other, they can get married. They will have dozens of problems, but it may work out. But what if they have little or no foundation of love? Forced marriages are very high risk. Marriage might create worse problems for all concerned—the innocent baby included. A shotgun wedding can shoot down a couple's chances for a happy life and bring misery to the child.

Abortion may be *an out* for some, but it may *be out* for others. It's out for Catholics and for others who believe that a new human being exists from the moment of conception. To them, it really would be murder—and that's a heavy load of guilt to carry for a whole lifetime. Moreover, unless it is done under proper conditions, abortion can be highly dangerous, even fatal.

Or she may have the baby outside of marriage, but then she has another difficult choice to make. If she gives the baby up for adoption, in some states she may never again see her child, never know who has it, never know if it's alive or dead. That may be best for her baby, but some women report that they continue to feel deep grief for years. Each time they see a child the right age, they wonder: Could that one be mine?

The other choice is to keep her baby herself. Studies show that those who go this route score lower on maturity tests than those who choose adoption, partly because it's often done for selfish reasons. And it can be a rough road. There is still a stigma placed on both the unwed mother and her child, especially in rural and small-town America. The woman's chances to marry are fewer. She often ends up on welfare—at taxpayers' expense. Or her parents may have to help with the child's care and training. In all, the girl's dream of keeping her child may turn out to be a tragic nightmare.

So that's the tale of two females. The contrast is stark and sobering. No woman ought to have to face an unwanted pregnancy. But if a couple is risking pregnancy, they'd better figure out what they will do when it occurs.

So where should sex play be halted before marriage? Some place short of that point where the girl has even the slightest chance of conceiving a child. Fun is fine as long as it doesn't spoil something better.

In view of all this—plus the "eleven known facts"—a lot of young people are concluding that sex before marriage just doesn't make good sense. It is *not* a disgrace to be a virgin. It is in fact being mighty smart.

Principle 4. *Set your own limit—and stick to it.* Since it is your body, you have the right and the duty to decide what you do with it. It's a big decision. The stakes are high. Since you have only one body and one life to live, you'll want to claim the very most that life can offer.

So when you decide what your limit will be, you'll want it to be a sound, sober choice. You'll want to think it through beforehand and not wait until you're breathing hard in a red-hot petting session. You'll want your mind to rule your emotions, not the other way around. Follow your head, not your passion. It's best to call a firm halt to the process before there's even the slightest risk that you might "lose your head"—and with it your virtue.

And resist that old rattlesnake—*peer pressure.* Never mind what the couple in the back seat is doing. They may do that and not get pregnant or contract an STD. You may do it in the front seat and get *both!*

The toughest test comes once you're engaged. After you're fully committed to each other, it may be hard indeed to keep from going all the way. That's why I recommend long courtships but short engagements. That way it's not so hard to wait. And remember: one out of three engaged couples break up without marrying. It just may happen to you.

## Let's Shape Up, Guys

Some males expect the female to be the one who puts the brakes on sex. But just because you're a guy, you are not excused from responsibility to set limits on your own sexual behavior. You have the duty to act responsibly just as much as the female has. If you want the woman you marry to be a virgin, you have no right to be other than virgin for her.

The old double standard is as old-fashioned as the Model T Ford. Why should it always be the woman who has to say "No!"? Why shouldn't we fellows take as much responsibility for our sperm as we expect her to protect her uterus? In fact, it may soon become a legal duty.

A law in Wisconsin will no doubt spread to other states, because it is only fair. That law holds the male (and/or his parents) fully liable for half the costs of a pregnancy. If she has an abortion, that will cost you a couple of hundred bucks. (You may have to mortgage your bicycle!) AND (put your hand on your billfold, guys) if she has the baby and keeps it, *you are liable for half the costs of rearing that baby to age 18!* We're talking tens of thousands of dollars here! Isn't that a pretty sobering thought? Better keep it in mind the next time you get that gleam in your eye.

Principle 5. *Couples who care, should share.* I'm a great believer in honesty in relationships. If you and another person come to care a great deal for each other, I think you should talk frankly about just how far you will go in sharing sexual affection. If you care enough about each other to want to go beyond casual kissing, then you know each other well enough to be frank about your feelings.

So before things go very far, talk it all over calmly in a serious, honest atmosphere. Let each other know how you feel. Decide together just where your limit is going to be. Then both of you should take equal responsibility to—as the cheerleaders say—"Hold that line! Hold that line!" If one of you threatens to lose control, then the other must call a halt.

But, alas, if the male is not man enough to assume his share of the burden, then the female must carry it all alone—fair or not. She's the one who, after all, may take home a package her folks didn't order from Sears!

# ... **12** .......

# Some Things
# You Should Know
# Before You Marry

*I* N this day when a huge fund of scientific facts on
sex can be found in any good library, there is no
excuse for being ignorant. Let's quickly review how babies
are made.

When a girl begins her menstruation or "periods," her
body will produce from her ovaries one egg or ovum about
once every 28 days. This ovum travels through the fallopian tubes to her uterus (womb).

If the ovum gets fertilized by joining a male sperm
while in the tubes, it descends and starts to grow in the
blood-enriched wall of the uterus. If the ovum is not
fertilized, it is dissolved and menstrual blood passes out
of the cervix or neck of the uterus. It goes through the
vagina and is discharged.

Male sperm are introduced into a woman's body
through her vagina, the larger opening at the lower end
of her vulva. The vulva is the visible portion of her genitals
or female organs. It is located between her upper thighs
and at the base of the trunk of her body. During intercourse the male inserts his erect penis into the woman's

vagina and ejaculates or expels semen or fluid containing sperm at the opening of the uterus. The sperm then swim through the woman's cervix and uterus and into the fallopian tubes. There they sometimes meet and fertilize the ovum.

If a woman's vagina has not been penetrated by a penis or some other object, she may have a membrane called a hymen. This hymen covers part of the vaginal opening. When it is ruptured, it may be quite painful for her. In extreme cases a woman may have such a tough hymen that it will not break. It may then have to be clipped by a doctor before intercourse is possible. In other cases a woman may have no hymen at all.

Once the ovum is fertilized by a single male sperm, it starts to grow in her uterus. She is pregnant. The fetus grows in her lower abdomen for about nine months. Then the muscles of the uterus start to contract. They squeeze the baby through the cervix and out the opening of the vagina. This is called labor and birth. Another human being is thus brought into the world.

## The "Favored Four"—or Six— Contraceptives

Many married couples choose to delay having children or decide they don't want children at all. Once you marry, you and your spouse must make this decision. Unless you're prepared for quick and repeated pregnancy, you need to know how to prevent it. Highly effective ways to prevent conception are now available. But none of them is perfect, and some may pose serious hazards to health.

As of now, the four contraceptive methods doctors and other experts commonly recommend are the oral pill, the IUD, the diaphragm with spermicidal jelly, and the condom. The first three are used by the female, and each of them requires the attention of a trained expert to be safe and effective. Let's discuss them in the order of probable effectiveness.[1]

## The Contraceptive Pill (About 89— 97½% Effective in Actual Practice)

The pill acts to control the chemistry of the woman's body. In effect, it fools her body into thinking she's already pregnant. She may even exhibit such symptoms as morning sickness. The pill must be taken each day without fail for a certain number of days—usually 20—then it is not taken for several days. The instructions should be followed to the letter.

The pill prevents the ovum from being expelled at the usual time—normally about 14 days before the onset of the woman's next period. When she stops taking the daily pill, she menstruates as usual and the cycle begins anew.

Women should never take birth control pills except under a doctor's care. Don't ever steal them out of mother's cupboard. They may kill you—literally. What is protection for one woman may be poison for another. Some women with special medical problems should never take the pill. For most it is safe, but some studies indicate a possible link with cancer in women who take the pill for many years.

## The Intrauterine Device or IUD (About 95% Effective, BUT—)

The IUD is a small, wirelike gadget that is placed in the uterus. It comes in many forms—T and L shapes are common. It may be of metal or plastic, and is especially effective if there is copper in it. The "shield" type is highly dangerous and is no longer legal. All types must be inserted by a medical specialist.

The best theory about how the IUD works seems to be that sperm go right through to the tubes. But even if the egg is fertilized, it does not attach itself to the uterine wall and grow. Perhaps the IUD acts as a "foreign body" and causes the rejection of the fertilized egg. This method is thus unacceptable for Roman Catholics, as is the "morning-after pill," since both cause a very early abortion of an already fertilized ovum.

An advantage of the IUD is that as long as it is in place, it needs no further attention. When the couple wants a child, the woman can simply have it removed. It is a highly effective birth control device. However, it can be very risky and in some cases fatal.

## The Diaphragm and Spermicidal Jelly (About 84—85% Effective)

The diaphragm has a large ring-shaped rim, with a thin, loose, supposedly airtight sheet of rubber or plastic across it. It must be carefully fitted by a physician and refitted after every pregnancy. The woman spreads a coat of spermicidal jelly in it and inserts it into the vagina before intercourse so that it fully covers the entrance to the womb. The sperm-killing jelly helps destroy any live sperm that try to swim around the edges of the diaphragm.

This method is also highly effective and safe, though one couple I know used it faithfully and still had three of their five babies unplanned. It has to be inserted each time before intercourse. If it is properly inserted, neither party is likely to be aware of its presence during coitus. It must be left in place for at least six to eight hours after intercourse. After each use it must be washed and prepared for a future use.

It is rated about 84% effective by Planned Parenthood, but 85% by the FDA (Food and Drug Administration).

## The Condom—Only if Tested (80—86% Effective)

Of the four most-used methods, the condom or "rubber" is the only one that is used by the male, is available with no doctor's prescription, and provides some protection against venereal disease. It is therefore the method most often used by sexually active young, unmarried couples.

The condom is a supposedly airtight covering that is rolled over the erect penis. It prevents sperm from reaching the vagina.

Latex (*not* "lambskin") condoms used with spermicide can be fairly effective—about 86%. But there is one catch. About 20% of them leak, according to former U.S. Surgeon General Koop. That means that they need to be carefully tested for such leaks, since these holes are usually too small to be seen easily. Sperm are so tiny that they can escape through the smallest of holes. Since most young users do not bother to test condoms, they are much less reliable.

A condom may be tested in two ways. It can be filled with water and examined for leaks. Or it can be inflated like a balloon and placed under water. If air bubbles appear anywhere, throw it away. (Sorry. No refunds!) The way many teens use condoms, they are only a startlingly 45% effective. Ashamed to go to local drugstores or to Planned Parenthood for the best brands, a young man may purchase condoms from slot machines in the men's john of a truck stop. He may then carry one around in his billfold, hoping he'll get a chance to use it. Every time he sits down, the billfold moves back and forth, producing wear on the condom. And where is the wear? Right near the end where there must not be any leaks.

## Rhythm—or "Safe Period" (84% Effective)

For the most part, the so-called safe period is highly unsafe—in spite of the recent claims of improvements. The theory is that there is a span of time just before and just after menstruation when the female cannot conceive. But the theory limps on a lot of legs. It is often hard to pinpoint the time of ovulation. Some emotional upset or strain may alter a woman's schedule. Sperm can live much longer in a favorable environment than once thought. The couple must abstain for long periods of time—perhaps at the very times when they least want to do so. For many women ovulation is not regular. All in all, the safe period just is not safe. The woman on the safe period method (thermal) is five times as likely to get pregnant as the woman on the pill. If she uses both thermal and mucus methods, pregnancy is still three times more likely. Other methods must be used if conception is to be dependably avoided.

There is one way to make this method more reliable. But both the man and woman must take a thorough training course on how to use the *combined* safe-period (thermal) and Billings (mucus detection) methods. If they practice them *faithfully and without exception,* this may be quite effective in averting conception.[2] But it means they must refrain from intercourse about half the time. And that can be rough! That's why that method hasn't caught on with too many couples.

## The Sponge (74—85% Effective)

This one is also approved by the FDA now. The sponge is saturated with spermicidal jelly; it fits in the vagina and covers the cervix. The low rate of effectiveness, plus some danger of Toxic Shock Syndrome if left in too long, leads some scientists (like myself) to discourage its use. All spermicides are about equally risky—only 74% effective.

## The Cervical Cap

Like the diaphragm and condom, this is a "barrier" method. The cap fits over the neck of the cervix in the vagina to bar entrance to the uterus.

The chart below provides a comparison of contraceptive success during the first year of use by teens vs. women overall.[3]

| Method | Overall | Teens |
|--------|---------|-------|
| Pill | 94% | 89% |
| Condom | 80–86% | 45–86% |
| Diaphragm | 84% | 84% |
| Rhythm | 84% | 69% |
| Spermicides | 74% | 74% |

Note that when *teens* use the pill or rhythm, they are about twice as likely to get pregnant as women in general using the same methods. The failure rate may also be much greater with the use of the condom.

## Unsafe at Any Speed

As of this writing, no other current methods of contraception are considered effective enough to count on.

Withdrawal of the penis before ejaculation is unsafe for two reasons. First, 40% of the time there is live sperm in the preseminal lubricant-like fluid that emerges from the end of the penis during sexual excitement. Second, since the male must pull away at precisely the time when he least wants to do so, he will likely overstay his welcome. He may wait too long and eject sperm into the vagina.

The douche, or washing out of the vagina, is of little value—whether one uses vinegar, Coca Cola, or whatever. Why? It takes only 20 seconds after ejaculation for live sperm to enter the cervix. A douche will likely be much too late to be of any help.

Foams are not reliable in and of themselves, though they may add a margin of safety when used with one of the "favored four" methods. Alone, they're only 74% effective.

Lack of sexual excitement in a woman is no help; she may be cold and unresponsive and still conceive. It happens quite often in rape cases.

The coital position used gives no protection either. As long as sperm gets into the vagina, the risk is great. Having sex in a sitting or standing position will not help at all.

In sum, no contraceptive is fully adequate. And even the "favored four" are not all that effective. The only sure way to avoid pregnancy is not to have intercourse at all. Put another way, the only 100% oral contraceptive is the word "No!"

## Assume That No *Means* No

Some males assume that when a female says *no*, she really means *maybe*, or even that (secretly) she really wants him to go ahead. No way. Take her at her word. Some men who do otherwise actually commit date rape—a vicious and horrible crime. And these days more and more women are taking men who do that to court.

On the other hand, women must also avoid "leading a man on" to the point where he assumes that she wants him to go all the way. Self-control is needed on *both* sides. But no matter what a woman says or does (or what kind of clothing she wears), rape is still rape and there is never any excuse for it.

Some young men are now complaining that some girls come on to them for sex. Women are now being shown on TV as the main aggressors. They lure, almost force, the male to have sex with them. That kind of behavior is no more acceptable for women than men. Women who do that are just asking for trouble, and a lot of men shy away from women who do that when it comes to choosing a wife. And the word gets around. Some men not only kiss and tell, they kiss and brag.

## Don't Get the Wrong Idea

Just because I've outlined the best available ways to avert pregnancy doesn't mean that I encourage premarital sex by the unmarried couple. In fact, I take quite the opposite view. In light of all the facts, I don't think it makes any sense at all to have full sex before you marry. It is dumb—really dumb—to take all those chances of fouling up your whole life for the sake of a few sexual thrills for the moment. But if you insist on being foolish enough to do it, for heaven's sake use your head as well as your tail! The evidence is clear and overriding: It is very easy to get pregnant. One out of every three unmarried teenage girls who becomes sexually active gets pregnant. Of these, one in five gets pregnant *the very first month she starts having sex!*

## So What Are the Choices?

Since going all the way to intercourse involves such serious risks, how can one deal with all those deep sexual urges? You have a number of options.

I do think you are very, very smart to reject premarital sex. There are just too many ways it can mess up your life now and in the future. It's far wiser to wait.

You can, of course, abstain. You can use willpower— or "won't power." No one *has* to have sex. Many go without having sex for years or even a lifetime without negative results. This has never been popular with the masses, but it's one option.

Another choice is to decide together how far down that "road to arousal" you (or you two) think you should go. Go no farther. Express your emotions up to that point, and then just call a halt.

Or you can "sublimate" the sex urges. That is, you can firmly decide to engage in some other kinds of things as a deliberate substitute for giving in to your sex drive. It could be sports, exercise, art, or some hobby—almost anything that really holds your interest. This can distract your attention away from thoughts of sex.

If you really want to save intimate sex for marriage, you can do it. It will help if you steer clear of the kinds of things that can tempt you. You can avoid the "R" or "X" types of movies, or books or magazines that are likely to arouse your sex urges. Try not to let yourself get into situations with your dates where having sex would be easy. Being with the person in a house when parents or others are not around, for instance. Or parking in lonely spots for long periods of time. Or double dating with couples who you think will have sex with each other in your presence. Exposing yourself to these kinds of situations is just asking for trouble.

And you can enlist the help of your home folks. Have a few rules such as:

● a definite time when you have to be in at night.

● be home within a certain amount of time after the end of a school function. (Allow time enough for a hamburger after the game, but not enough time to park and "spark" in some lonely spot.)

● you and your date are not to be in each other's home alone when parents are not present. (That's the place where most young people now have sex their first time.)

● leave an outside light on until you're home safely.

Look upon such rules as clear evidence that your folks really do love you and care what happens to you, rather than as an undue restriction on your freedom.

## What about Masturbation?*

One other option to help cope with sex urges is masturbation. It does give full sexual satisfaction to most people, especially men.

Masturbation is touching or rubbing one's own sex organs for pleasure. A person may or may not reach a sexual climax (called an orgasm) in the process. This brings a peak of pleasure when it happens. A male orgasm is called an ejaculation, since spurts of fluids called *semen* will emerge from the end of the erect penis. Males who masturbate almost always have an orgasm.

Sex feelings can come at a very young age. Even small children may masturbate.

For a number of reasons men tend to masturbate much more often than women. One reason is that most are not

*Some of the material for this section is from my book, *Sex, Dating and Love: 77 Questions Most Often Asked* (Minneapolis: Augsburg, 1984), pp. 113-120.

married or living-in at the time they are at their peak of sexual interest—at ages 17 to 19. By age 28, when women reach their peak of interest, most women are married. I've already mentioned some other reasons why male sex interest is normally more quickly aroused.

Another point is that a male will get an erection about once every hour or two while he is sleeping. If he wakes up with one, he may go ahead and masturbate. In any case, scientists have found that about 94% of all males masturbate quite regularly before they marry, unless they are sexually active. By contrast, only about 63% to 80% of females masturbate *at some time* before they marry.

Will it harm you if you do it? As of now I know of no scientific proof at all that masturbation will harm a person. It does not seem to affect the body, mind, nerves, or emotions.

There are a lot of myths about this subject, though. We were once told that doing it would make you go blind. Or make hair grow in the palm of your hand. Or make you go insane. That is nonsense. Masturbation does not affect one's mind—with one exception: If you worry a lot about it or feel deep guilt. Extreme worry or guilt about anything can affect a person's mental health.

I once knew of such a case. A very religious boy of 13 was convinced that "playing with himself—down there" was an unforgivable sin. Yet he could not seem to stop doing it. He was overcome with guilt feelings. He'd actually cry himself to sleep after doing it, convinced that he was going straight to hell! How sad.

As a youth I was told that masturbation would make one's face break out in pimples. It won't. When an adolescent's body chemistry is changing, it is quite normal for the face to have blemishes. But there was always some nosey neighborhood gossip who would watch the faces of teenagers. If she saw one who had such blemishes she'd raise an accusing eyebrow. "I know what you're doing," she'd seem to say. Well, she may have been right. But the masturbation had nothing to do with the pimples.

Nor is masturbating "self-abuse." In no way does it abuse or do damage to a person. Another myth is that if you masturbate while single it will ruin your sex life after you're wed. It won't. Once you have the chance to have full intercourse with your mate, you'll not likely do a lot of masturbating. You'll have a much better way to deal with your urges.

All these myths were of course scare tactics to try to keep the young people from masturbating. But as of now, science has found no harmful results, unless the person worries about it.

Two minor cautions might be in order, however. If a girl inserts an object into her vagina while masturbating, it could cause infection. Or if a person masturbates too often or too much at one time, it may cause some temporary loss of feeling in the sex organs. That is called sexual anesthesia. But no problem. The full feeling will come back in a short time if you just stop doing it for awhile.

If you masturbate, will it make you become gay or lesbian? I know of no evidence at all that supports this view. We just don't know yet what makes an adult person prefer others of the same sex. Some people think it's brought on due to certain kinds of relations with parents or siblings. Some think the tendency may be inherited. Some think it may be learned as a child through group masturbation—or masturbating another person—or oral or other sex experiments. We just don't know. As of now there is no evidence that masturbation is a factor at all in homosexuality.

Until we find out for sure that homosexuality is not a learned behavior, it is probably smart not to experiment with same-sex sexual practices. Of course, it's just fine to have *real good friends* of the same sex, so long as it does not rob you of your healthy interest in persons of the opposite sex. (It is, of course, quite normal for a young person to prefer friends of the same sex before reaching puberty.)

Now what about religion? Is masturbation a sin? The Bible does not say. But if you fall short of what *you* feel you ought to do or what you feel God wants you to do, then you sin in your own eyes. For example, if you have been taught that to masturbate is bad, then you will feel that it's wrong.

However, most of the major Protestant churches in America have no official church statements on the subject. They don't seem too worried about it. The same is true for some Catholic leaders. A priest once told me, "Our church considers it a sin, but not very much." His point was this: If one has fantasies about another person while masturbating, it might be a sin for two reasons. First, the person might be tempted to make that fantasy come true. Second, Jesus said, "Anyone who looks at a woman [or man?] lustfully has already committed adultery with her in his heart."[4] That is, you may see the person not as a living, feeling, worthy human being, but largely as a sex object to be used for your own selfish lust.

However, it must be noted that other Catholic leaders—and some Protestant ones—take a different view. For example, the Vatican views masturbation as a serious sin. Sex is seen as a gift of God to be shared, but only in marriage. It has a twofold purpose in a marriage: for procreation and as a means of mutual sharing of love between spouses. Since masturbation centers the sex expression on the self, it is thought to be an abuse of the purpose of sex. It is not that masturbation is evil or bad in itself. It's just that it violates the principle that sex is to be shared, and only with one's spouse. That is the official Catholic view of the purpose of sex.

Still another view of masturbation is taken by some leaders of various religions. They argue that masturbation for pleasure is not wrong in itself unless someone is being hurt by it. They hold that God created human beings to be sexual persons for three reasons, not just one or two. Certainly sex is for the all-important role of procreation. We share that with all the rest of God's creatures. But two facts, they think, prove that God created human sexuality for two other reasons as well: (1) for personal pleasure, and (2) as a unique way for two married persons to join their total personalities into a joyful sharing of their love for each other.

One evidence they cite is that human beings are the only species that is created so that we usually engage in sex in a face-to-face love embrace. Did God make a mistake in creating us that way? Or did God intend for us to use sex also as a way of sharing love in marriage?

The other evidence to support this view is that, unique among all creatures, human females are the only ones who will permit, and may even want, sex at times other than when they can conceive. Every other female species rejects the male except when she is ready to conceive. Again, did God make a mistake? Or did God mean to make human sexuality something to share with joy with our married mate?

Those who follow this line of reasoning hold that the Lord made no mistake. God planned it exactly that way— and it is good. Therefore, they reason, masturbation for pleasure also is not wrong, just so long as it does not hurt anyone else.

A further point. One important role our sex urge plays is to make us notice and make friends with those of the opposite sex. It nudges us in their direction. That is good.

But if one masturbates too much, that urge may be decreased. The result? No nudging. As one girl put it in the film, *Sexuality and Communications*,[5] "You don't meet too many nice people that way."

All in all, it seems doubtful that masturbation is considered to be much of a sin by your religion. But check it out with your priest, minister, bishop, or rabbi. If your religion is against it, you will likely feel guilty if you do it.

To sum up, masturbation may not be a good choice for those who feel it is a serious sin, or for those who would worry a lot about it. Others have used it as an out, since it does take the edge off of the desire.

It would seem, however, that if it's a choice between masturbating and giving in to unwed intercourse, the former would do much less harm. Any damage that might be done would be only to one's self.

Premarital sex, on the other hand, does harm to you, your partner, and to your marriage chances. If there is a pregnancy, it will be also harmful to the unborn life, to your friends and families, and to your whole future. If you get AIDS or some other sexually transmitted disease, it could ruin your health, even kill you. It's your choice to make, but of the many options open to you, it would seem premarital sex is the worst one of them all.

It isn't easy to say no but these two thoughts just may help. When one nonvirgin girlfriend tried to convince her virgin pal to give in to sex the girl replied: "I can be like you any time I choose—but you can never ever again be like me."

It may also help to keep in mind what a woman once wrote to the "Dear Abby" newspaper column: "You often receive letters from young girls asking: 'Should I or should I not go all the way before marriage?' I was given a beautiful reason why I should not, and I never forgot it. There were no heavy warnings or confusing explanations. It was simply this: 'Intimacy between man and woman is God's wedding gift to the newlyweds, and [this] gift is not to be opened early.' "

Good luck. I hope you make the choice that is the very best and most sensible one for you.

## But What if I'm No Longer a Virgin?

Many have already had, or are still having, unwed sex. Can you get back on track and erase some, perhaps most of, the damage that may have been done? Yes, you certainly can. So don't give up.

Here's the good news. If you stop doing it, the longer you refrain from it, the less most of these negatives will apply to you. You cannot regain your physical virginity. But you can become a "psychological virgin" by turning your life around and saying "NO!" from this point on.

Of course, you may not be able to repair all the damage that may already be done—like an STD or pregnancy— but you can most certainly reshape your future in a new direction any time you so decide. Resolve to put your past behind you and go on from here. It won't be easy, but you can do it if you set your mind and will to it.

Now let's return to the remaining key clues to distinguish real love from infatuation and sexual attraction.

# ... 13 ...

## CLUE SEVEN:
## How Do You
## See Each Other?

*T* HERE are two aspects of this clue. One has to do
with the effect of your romance on your relationships with other people. The other deals with your ability
to think straight about the object of your affections and
your relationship.

### Signs of Infatuation

When infatuated, *you live in a one-person world.* Your
attraction is like the earth's attraction to the sun—your
whole universe revolves around that other person. Nothing else matters. No one else is as important. You are all
wrapped up in each other—perhaps literally! When infatuated, you tend to neglect your family and pay little
or no attention to your other friends. You turn a deaf ear
to your teachers or your boss. You fail to do your homework. You lose interest in things that used to excite you.

Both of you tend to home in on that one relationship.
It becomes not only the most important thing in your
world, but the only thing that really matters to you. Your

relationship tends to be exclusive. Your other friends feel left out, neglected, or ignored.

Since this "romantic love" (infatuation) is of such central concern to you, nothing must be allowed to stand in its way. You think you're justified in giving up anything in favor of this amazing event that has happened so unexpectedly.

One married woman with three children reports that within 48 hours after she first met a certain man at a lodge convention, she would have gone to bed with him. As it happened, they were both happy in their own marriages. Even so, she might have left her family and gone off with him, if he had pressed her to do so.

That couple was lucky. In a few weeks their ardor cooled and reason rescued them from their romantic emotions. Yet after many years they still have warm feelings toward each other. Many others are not so fortunate. They act rashly in the name of "love" and rue the day. But the damage is already done.

## Signs of Love

As with infatuation, in real love the beloved may well be the most important person in the world to you. But here's the big difference. In real love, you *expand* your world to include the beloved.

If you really love each other, you don't abandon or neglect your other relationships. Instead, you just *add this wonderful new relationship to all the others you have*. It becomes a plus, not a replacement.

You still maintain good ties with your family, your friends, your teachers. You retain your interest in your work or studies—assuming that you had such an interest in the first place. Things that you liked to do before, you still like to do. Your world grows larger, not narrower.

## Is Your Beloved Faultless?

Romantic infatuation is a vaccine that immunizes you against seeing anything wrong with the other person. *You tend to put your beloved on a pedestal as a paragon of perfection.* You live in a kind of romantic Disneyland.

No one can tell you anything wrong about the object of your affections. At best, you won't believe it. At worst, you may turn against the accuser in anger and rejection.

"You know, Bob," says a worried Dad, "I think that girl is a gossip. You should have heard what she said about her brother's wife."

"You don't understand her, Dad," counters Bob, dashing to the defense. "She's not a gossip. She just likes people!" Or Mom may say, "Judy, I think your young man is a drunk. When I saw him last night in town, he could hardly stand up. If it hadn't been for the lamppost, he'd have fallen flat on his face in the gutter."

"Oh, no, Mom," she chirps. "He never gets drunk. He just gets to feeling good!" If Mom could buy that young man for his actual worth and sell him for what Judy thinks he's worth, Mom would be a millionaire.

If you're infatuated, you defend the other person against all critics. You just will not admit that he or she has any faults. This is idealization. You idealize not only each other, but also your situation. You two may have gross problems and obstacles to cope with—different religions, hopes, values, family, and cultural backgrounds. Danger signals by the dozen! Yet you are not concerned. You don't even feel the need to think about these enormous hazards before marriage. You think that somehow it all just has to come out OK. Your great "love" will see you through.

The tendency to idealize is very strong in our culture. Elsie King found that two-thirds of the women and more than half the men she studied had unrealistic or false views of the person they were about to wed.[1]

What makes us idealize so much? For one thing, we tend to be on our best behavior while courting. We show only our best side. Another reason is the "halo effect," or the tendency to judge the whole personality largely in terms of one or two highly admired qualities. One great trait or two can fool us into thinking that the whole person is great as well.

And sex gets into the act, too. One study showed that male subjects who were sexually aroused rated the pictures of the same girls to be much more attractive than did the same males when they were not aroused. The greater his sexual need, the better the girl looked to the male.[2] *So it is with infatuation. You'll tend to see what you want to see—* and need to see—in the other person, rather than what is really there. (By the way, this is another reason not to get too sexually aroused.)

*If it's love, on the other hand, you admit their faults but love the person in spite of them.* You will idealize the other person to some degree, even in real love. It is a matter of how much and what kind.

In infatuation, you tend to project what you want to see onto the other. You create the ideal, even if the elements of the ideal are not there. In love, you see the person's real merits and build on that. A mutual process is set in motion. Your love leads you to appreciate the best in the other. In turn, as the other person learns of your love, it brings out the best in her or him. You are frank to admit that the other is not perfect. But you see so much to be admired and respected that you can live with those faults.

## Is Love Blind?

No, but infatuation is. Infatuation, like other extreme emotions such as anger, hate, and fear, distorts thinking. It is most deceptive. Infatuated persons prefer feeling to thinking. Only the passing of time will bring about gradual return to reality. When the ideal bubble bursts—and burst it will—pain and disillusionment sets in.

Again, it pays to be honest. Much of the pain and tragedy of romantic infatuation could be avoided if the couple would level with themselves and with each other. Instead, they hide their faults and mislead the other into thinking they are something they are not.

For this they pay an awful price. "Perhaps the most important reason for self-disclosure is that without it we cannot truly love. How can I love a person I don't know? How can the other person love me if he doesn't know me?" These questions posed by Sidney Jourard and Ardis Whitman are food for thought. Their answer? That honesty is a must.[3]

In this sense, they suggest that we behave like small children and "act our real selves." Perhaps this is what Jesus meant when he said one must become as a little child to enter the kingdom of God. It may also be the way to enter the kingdom of love.

Time is the infatuated person's best friend. It is both the great revealer and the great healer. When your heart has been broken, time will heal the hurt.

Time also is the best antidote for the deadly poison of idealization. "As interaction increases, knowledge converts the dream image into awareness of the real partner. Awareness punctures the dream bubble and brings the relationship down to earth."[4] Time can shield you from plunging into an unsound marriage on the strength of a mere infatuation. Love that is time tested is the real thing.

# ... **14** .......

## CLUE EIGHT:
## How Do Others
## View You Two?

*N* OBODY loves you more than your friends and your folks. They care what happens to you. It's important how they feel. So what do your friends and parents think about your relationship?

We often hear some young person say: "Why should it matter to us if other people don't approve of our romance? After all, we're marrying each other, not each other's families and friends."

That is in part true, but in a very real sense you *do* marry your mate's family and friends. You marry all that he or she identifies with and cares about. That includes friends and family.

### Signs of Infatuation

If you are infatuated, chances are that *few or none of your family and friends approve* of your relationship. Your beloved's friends likely don't think much of you, and your friends aren't very fond of him or her, either. They may not come right out and say it to your face, but they wish you'd "hurry up and come to your senses."

In infatuation, each of you will also dislike the other's friends. He may think—if not say—that he can hardly stand to be around "those idiots she calls her friends." And she may wonder what possible good he sees in "that bunch of baboons" he runs around with.

All of this can be a warning signal. You will do well to think carefully before you marry.

## Signs of Love

If it's love, *most or all friends and parents approve.* You like each other's friends and feel comfortable with them, because you have a good deal in common. In rare cases a "best friend" may feel jealous, hence resentful of the time you two "love birds" spend together. But for the most part, there is mutual acceptance and friendliness.

Why do friends tend to approve when it's real love and not approve if it's infatuation? If you've taken geometry you may recall one of the main postulates: "Things equal to the same thing are equal to each other." That applies to this clue.

Over the years, both you and your beloved have developed a circle of friends of the same sex. Now ask yourself: What brings friends of the same sex together? If you are heterosexual you choose same-sex friends not on the basis of sexual attraction, but because of their personalities and because you have lots of interests in common. You like to talk about and do many of the same things.

In infatuation, you have been drawn to each other largely by physical attraction. This is completely different from what attracted you to your same-sex friends. Therefore, since the two of you have few interests in common, few if any of your friends approve of your choice.

On the other hand, if you really love each other, your relationship is also based on the many interests you share. You are friends as well as lovers. Now remember. Things equal to the same thing are equal to each other. Since you like in each other the same kinds of things you like in your friends of the same sex, then all of you have a great deal in common. You all have lots to talk about, many of the same interests, a great many similar ideas. Thus you are all far more likely to get along well together. So most or all of your friends will approve of your relationship.

Judson T. and Mary Landis have summarized this idea.

> Two who love each other must be friends in the same sense that any two people of the same sex are friends. This means they enjoy each other's company because of genuine congeniality, aside from sexual interest; they want to confide in each other, to talk things over, and to share amusement, ideas, disappointment or grief. They tend to see life through each other's eyes. They are at ease and comfortable with each other, as good friends always are.[1]

So if few or none of your friends approve of your boy or girl friend, beware. Your "love" interest is probably based on physical attraction and sex. But if many friends approve, that suggests that you have much mutuality, many things in common. These factors are basic elements in a real love relationship. It follows, then, if most of your friends approve, you are more likely in love.

Kelly suggests several thoughtful questions to ask yourself. "Can you be yourself naturally with the person you love? Does he or she bring out the best in you, or the worst? Are you genuinely proud of [this person]? Do you enjoy being with him [or her] in the company of your family and friends?"[2]

To these queries we would add one more. Are the same qualities present in your beloved that you like in your same-sex friends? If they are not present, proceed with caution. It may be just infatuation, not love.

## Do Parents and Family Approve?

Whether your home folks approve of your romance is another key part of this clue. When parents do not approve of a marriage, the failure rates are very high.

Most parents love their children. If you are a teenager, you may find that hard to believe. They may not let you have movie money or the car keys as often as you'd like. You may not get to stay out as late as you want. Still, mature parents want to see their children happy, both now and in the future. Your parents probably want you to have all the good things that life can bring. That includes a happy marriage.

So if your parents think you're about to make a big mistake, they are likely to oppose it. They don't want you to get hurt, to be robbed of future joy. If they're convinced you're making a poor choice, they just may be right. Since they don't have stars in their eyes like you do, they may be able to see the situation more clearly than you can. If so, then they are being your friends, not your enemies, by showing their concern or by not approving of the relationship.

There is one exception to this. In a few cases, parents may not be emotionally grown up, not willing or able to release sons or daughters to live their own lives. No girl is ever quite good enough for darling Jimmy. Or if sister brought home the angel Gabriel himself, Dad would find fault with him. In such cases, if the young person is ever to marry he or she must do so against the parent's wishes. But such cases are rare.

So if your parents object, be very sure it is they who are immature and not yourself before moving ahead. You may just be looking for an excuse to believe that they are wrong and you are right. You may be kidding yourself again.

It's usually a mistake for parents to "lay down the law" and forbid their children to see the person they object to. That will probably just drive the couple into each other's arms. They may resolve to show their folks what's what, so they'll slip out and meet anyway. This is known as the Romeo-and-Juliet effect, since these famed lovers had families who staunchly opposed their courtship. Studies have shown that parental opposition may actually cause a couple to fall deeper into "romantic love" or infatuation.[3] In time, this effect usually wears off, however, so don't marry foolishly just to spite your parents. You'd be cutting off your nose to spite your face.

## Scientific Support

There is strong evidence that peer and parental approval tend to indicate love. Harvey J. Locke once compared complaints registered by happily married persons with those of divorced individuals. Divorced persons were almost four times as likely to complain that they and their spouses had no mutual friends. That is, they seemed to have little in common with the other's friends. Locke also found that happily married couples were far less likely to have problems with each other's parents. Divorced men were three times as likely to list "interference of in-laws" as a major complaint.[4] This bears out the view that real loves are more likely to gain the approval of parents.

So be alert to note what others think of your choice.
When most friends and parents object, take special care.
They are trying to tell you something you should know.

But if most or all of them approve, that is a good sign.
Take heart. And the more there are who approve, the
more likely it is that you've found real love.

## ... 15 ........

# CLUE NINE:
# What Does
# Distance Do?

*M* ANY things can separate a young couple. Families move away, young people go off to school or work or military service. If you're apart, you may feel anxious as well as sad. "What if one of us finds someone else?" you may worry.

Will your interest in each other pull through the strain, or will it die out? These concerns are not without cause. Studies show that engaged couples are more likely to break up if they're separated.[1]

### Signs of Infatuation

If it is infatuation, absence makes the heart grow fonder—of somebody else! In infatuation Sue and Sam have been interested mainly in each other's physical equipment. That is, what they can see, hear, smell, taste or touch about each other. Such interest is hard to sustain when they're separated by a thousand miles. Since only a few things attract them to each other, the roots of the relationship are thin. It won't last long unless it gets nourished by a lot of face-to-face contact.

After the infatuated couple is apart for a few days or weeks, they begin to lose interest. It's not much of a thrill to kiss a photograph goodnight. After a while the physical equipment of some more available person begins to look good to them. So *if it is infatuation, it will die with distance.* It cannot survive the added strain of separation.

## Signs of Love

*Love survives separation. It may even grow.* Absence does indeed make the heart grow fonder. Why? Because love is rooted in attraction to the other's total personality, not just physical appeal. When you are in love, a great many of the tendrils of your personalities tend to grow together, to unite you into loving oneness. When you have to be apart, you are not your whole self. When the other person is not there, *you* are not all there. Something vital is missing, and you long to be reunited. You realize how much your relationship means to you.

So if a separation comes, don't worry about it. If you do find that it's infatuation and hence doesn't survive, be grateful—it's a good thing you found out before it was too late. On the other hand, if you survive the separation, it may be a good clue that it's real love.

# ... 16 ........

## CLUE TEN: How Do Quarrels Affect the Romance?

*E* VEN a couple united by love will quarrel once in a while. Any time two people seek to merge the many facets of their personalities, there will be rough edges to iron out. That is to be expected.

So be prepared for some friction even if you're in love. You will disagree on a few things. Some aspects of your lives won't fit together well, at least not right away. There will be many adjustments to make, and sparks may fly at times until you get things worked out between you.

Sometimes a couple will tell me, "We've been married 20 years and never had a quarrel." Well, bless their angelic little hearts! When I hear that, I suspect that one of three things is true.

First, they may be lying through their teeth. They've quarreled and they know it. They just won't admit it.

Second, they quite honestly may have forgotten. Over the years a couple may well discover more creative and constructive ways to settle disputes. They may learn to tether tongues and fetter feelings. They don't argue, they discuss. They learn the art of give and take. So since it may have been many years since they last quarreled, they may have forgotten that they ever did.

Third, if a couple have in fact been married 20 years and never had a quarrel, at least one of them is probably a "Milquetoast"—a doormat who does not stand up for his or her own personal rights. That's not a marriage. One dominates, the other just submits.

So the important thing is not whether you quarrel, but the way you quarrel. Ask yourself three questions. (1) How severe are our quarrels? (2) How often do they occur? (3) What is the final effect of quarrels on our relationship? The answers are good indicators of the nature of your romance.

## Signs of Infatuation

In infatuation, *quarrels will kill the relationship, and they tend to become more frequent and more severe*. Since your main attraction is physical and the number of interests you hold in common are few, the few things you do have in common soon prove too weak to give lasting support. The fabric of your romance starts to wear thin. You begin to lose interest. You find yourselves disagreeing on more and more things, so more and more often you quarrel. The words get more harsh and full of mean barbs. You hurt each other more and more deeply—and you may even do it on purpose.

After each quarrel, you kiss and make up. (That part is oh, so wonderful, be it love or infatuation.) But your renewed closeness does not last. The bonds between you continue to go to pieces. Finally, the sour times over-shadow the sweet. One or both of you decide that it's not worth the struggle. Hard as it is to do so, you break it off. You may go back together a time or two, but there are no bonds of love. In time, you break for good and go your separate ways. Be glad, not sad! You're lucky you had it happen before you were wed, because happen it would.

## Signs of Love

If it is love, the opposite is true. *Love lives through quarrels, and quarrels become less frequent and less severe.* A loving couple has a broader base of things in common. Their relationship can absorb a good deal of strain because it has a firmer foundation.

In love you feel more a part of each other, so you have more of a stake in working things out. You see a future together and seek to claim it. You try harder to find good substitutes for conflict. You learn to communicate in more creative ways.

For instance, you can learn to discuss frankly without arguing. Nobody wins an argument; it just confirms both of you more solidly in your own views. One couple makes it a practice never to reply in anger, no matter how great the urge to do so. "Just as it takes two to tango, it takes two to tangle," the girl explained. "When one of us gets angry, the other just shuts up until the dust settles. It works, too."

"I'm sorry" may well be the hardest words you'll ever say. But atonements bring at-homeness. It is only common courtesy to show others that we regret a past mistake. Such an admission will likely call forth warm acceptance and response in kind from the other person. Does love really mean never having to say you're sorry? On the contrary, we should never take the forgiveness of another for granted, no matter how deep the love bond between us. Maybe our loved one does not *demand* that we say it, but it will be much appreciated if we do.

So quarrels, while common, are not crucial. There are other ways to settle disputes, and loving couples need to find them.

## Constructive Quarreling

Some writers hold that conflict is not only normal, but necessary. They even offer rules on how to fight. I doubt this is the best approach for the average couple.

However, conflict between two people who love each other can serve a useful purpose. Quarrels can be constructive. An electrical fuse serves to keep a sudden burst of strong current from blowing out the whole power system. In the same way, an occasional quarrel will cause brief grief, but it may avert even greater marital damage. It may be better to blow off some steam and spoil an evening than to blow the whole relationship.

Jim and Jill have been married for some months. Each of them has found a few frustrating faults in the other. Jim hides behind his paper at breakfast when she'd like to talk, and Jill talks with her mother a lot by phone. They find these things somewhat irritating, but say nothing. After all, they love each other and do not wish to offend.

Then one day Jim comes home after a bad day at the office. (You know the old story. Dad gets chewed out by his boss, he comes home and fusses at Mom, Mom yells at Jeffy, and Jeffy goes out and kicks the dog.) Jill is on the phone with you-know-who—and the soup is starting to scorch.

Jim explodes. "Good heavens, woman! Can't you stop talking to that mother of yours long enough to get a decent meal?" Jill's jaw drops. Hurt and shocked, she bangs down the receiver.

"Well, if you'd come out from behind your stupid paper once in a while, I wouldn't need to talk to Mom so much," she shoots back. Then the argument really heats up.

Before long they calm down and feel sorrow and shame. They embrace. Each one tries to take full blame for the outburst. Soon all is well again.

All may be well—but all is not the same. What has happened that may be a plus for their future together? For one thing, they leveled with each other. They brought their gripes out in the open instead of bottling them up.

Resentment and tensions may build up and fester into more serious problems. "Unless you say 'ouch,' your partners cannot know that they are stepping on your toes."[1] Now that Jim and Jill have alerted each other to things that bother them, they are likely to avoid doing those same things so much in the future.

## Quarrels Can Be Dangerous

While they may do some good, quarrels can also do a lot of harm. Some studies show that quarrels may act more as a hair trigger than a safety valve. Murray Strauss found that as an argument heats up, so do the chances that the couple will resort to body blows.[2] If she throws a harsh remark at him, she's more likely to follow it up with the frying pan. This would scarcely qualify as a constructive quarrel.

Perhaps the key to constructive conflict is mutual caring and respect. A principle of child rearing could apply here. If a child ever has to be spanked, it should be done out of love, never out of anger or spite. The punishment should indeed hurt the parent as much as the child— though maybe not in the same place!

So it should be with marital quarrels. When the couple talks straight with each other, there should never be any doubt about an underlying bond of love. Each should be quite sure that the other deeply cares and is supportive, not destructive. The quarrel should not leave the partners hostile, hurt, angry, or bitter. The motive is to make the relationship better, not tear it down or destroy it—and each other.

## If You Break Up, Wake Up!

Some couples tend to break up and then get back together over and over. They can't seem to get along with—or without—each other for very long at a time. This is more likely to happen if they are involved with sex.

Sound the alarm bell! Most alert counselors know that if a couple breaks up and gets back together more than once during courtship, it's a bad sign. The couple should take fair warning. If it keeps happening before the wedding, it's likely to follow that same pattern afterward—and get worse. Who wants to put up with that for the rest of their lives?

# ... **17** ........

## CLUE ELEVEN: How Do You Feel about and Refer to Your Relationship?

*T* HIS is a very subtle clue. You will have to catch yourself off guard to apply it. But if you succeed, it will tell you how you feel about the other person in your subconscious or inner mind. It will help you unmask any play-acting you may unwittingly be doing in relation to each other. That way you can avoid fooling yourself— and the other person, too.

### Inner Feelings Are Revealing

Your deep inner feelings can be detected by observing closely the way you refer to yourself, to your beloved, and to your relationship. If you have trouble applying this test to yourself, alert a good friend to do it for you. Here's how it works.

Suppose that you have a sister who thinks she's found her Mr. Wonderful. You're still up when she comes in from their date. She has a stardust look in her eyes. You know the answer, but you ask anyway:

"How was your date?"

"Oh," she sighs, "just great. He's the most wonderful guy in the whole world."

Now's your chance. Play it cool and draw her out. "Oh?" you say innocently. "Tell me all about it." Then note with great care the words she uses to refer to herself and her young man. She may not tell you *all* about her date, but see if you can learn whether she's really in love from *what* she says and the *way* she says it.

"Well," your unsuspecting sister says, "he came to pick me up at a quarter past eight. He was supposed to come at eight, but he was late as usual. I didn't want him to think I was just waiting around for him, so I pretended I wasn't ready yet. I didn't go down for a full ten minutes.

"Out at his car, do you know what? He opened the door for me! 'Well,' I said, 'chivalry isn't dead!'

" 'Oh, yes it is,' he said. 'I just forgot.' I nearly died laughing. He's so clever.

"Well, I really liked that movie. It's just the kind I like best. Lots of creepy, crawly spiders and snakes.

" 'Are you afraid?' he whispered.

"I said, 'Oh, not when I'm with you, John.' And he squeezed me so hard I had to cough!

"After the movie I said I was hungry, so he took me to the drive-in. He had a hot dog with soya sauce and I had a hamburger with Limburger cheese and . . ." Yuck!

End of story. Now what are you hearing—besides an awful menu? How was she referring to him, to herself, and to the date? What were the key words she used?

## Signs of Infatuation

Time and again she used the words *I*, *me*, *my*, and *he*, *him*, *his*. She did not once use words like *we*, *us*, or *our*. She was unwittingly revealing her true feelings. By the use of these terms she has betrayed that she is still keeping her own identity carefully separate from his. It was "I did this" and "he said that" and "this happened to me (or to him)."

That tells us that she has not yet come to think of herself as part of a couple. She has not yet invested her self in the relationship. She's still clinging to her own selfish identity. That points to infatuation.

## Signs of Love

Two persons who have real love, on the other hand, come to feel that they are no longer separate, but have in great measure become one. Since they see themselves as a unit, as a couple, they tend to use *we* and *us* and *our* when they refer to what happens to them. It seems only natural and right to do so. They don't even have to think about it.

Reik cites an example from Asia to illustrate this merging of two persons into a kind of oneness.

Kuan Tao–Sheng, the wife of the great Chinese painter Chao Mang–Fu, felt that her husband had withdrawn his affection from her and bestowed it upon a mistress. She wrote this poem:

> Take a lump of clay,
> Wet it, pat it,
> Make a statue of you
> And a statue of me.
> Then shatter them, clatter them,
> Add some water,
> And break them and mold them
> Into a statue of you
> And a statue of me.
> Then in mine, there are bits of you

And in you there are bits of me.
Nothing ever shall keep us apart.[1]

Kuan Tao–Sheng won again the affection of her husband.

The couple truly in love are no longer two, but one, or rather two *in* one. "It is not implied that the two personalities disappear in this union," J. L. Hirning points out. "They are simply so much alike in motivation, attitudes, values, interests, and viewpoints that the differences between them are reduced to a minimum. There results a strong feeling of oneness; each person feels fully accepted, protected, and secure." They are still unique, separate persons, but they merge themselves into a pattern of common bonds. In this sense they have become "unselfed."[2]

## Love Is a Paradox

A paradox is something that sounds like a lie—a contradiction—but it is actually a great truth. Love is just such a paradox. In love, the couple gives up much of their separate selves, yet by doing so each becomes even more fulfilled as a self. A person's identity is not stifled by love; it is enriched. As they become a "we," each is at once a more fulfilled "I." They get double enjoyment out of everything they do. In the first place, each of them enjoys things as individuals just as they did before they were in love. But in addition, they have the added joy of sharing those things with the loved one.

At the University of Wisconsin–Platteville, my third-story office window faced west. When I'd spot a beautiful sunset I would call Jeannette, my wife, so she could enjoy it too.

The other side of the coin is that you may not want to do or enjoy things by yourself, unless the beloved is able to share them. "I don't want to go unless you can go, too, dear," is a common response of lovers. Real love is happiest when "we" do things together, not separately. Your own joy is incomplete unless you can share it with your love, either at the time or later.

# CLUE TWELVE:
# Are You Selfish
# or Selfless?

*C* LUES 12 and 13 may well be the two most important in the list. They have to do with whether a couple are self-centered or other-centered. They deal with the basic, core attitude that each person displays toward the other. Such elements will be crucial to the success or failure of any marriage.

## Signs of Infatuation

Why does Mike like to date Kate? She's the school's Homecoming Queen! Not that he likes her all that much. She is pretty and popular, but she's also spoiled and selfish. Still, he likes to date her because, since she's the "queen" of the school, dating her makes him the "king." He's the envy of all the fellows when they see him out with her. So he dates her, not for herself, but for the boost it gives to *his* ego.

If you are infatuated, *your ego response to the other person is mainly selfish and restrictive*. Your prime interest in the relationship is what it does for *you*. Infatuated persons say, "I really feel important when I'm with him" or "She really turns me on." The stress is selfish. They don't think about—or perhaps care—whether the other person's desires or needs are being filled. The key concern is that the person's own needs are served.

Other remarks that suggest selfishness are:

"I'm happier when I'm with him than I am with any other boy."

"If you loved me, you'd let me have sex with you."

"I'm not sure you could make me happy for the rest of my life."

"I know you love to dance (or watch football), but I don't—so I don't see why we should go to the prom (or game)."

Maybe you know someone who keeps a guy "on the string." She doesn't care much for him, treats him like dirt. But his devotion to her builds up her self-image.

Then there's the guy who keeps wanting to make his partner over to suit himself. He is not content that she be herself. He wants to change her into the person he wants or needs her to be. These are both examples of selfish infatuation.

It's not wrong for you to have your personal needs filled. Every person needs that. But when your overriding interest is your own selfish wants and needs, when you have little or no concern for the wants and needs of your partner—then that's not love. It's infatuation.

## Selfish Sex

Some guys date girls just for the thrill of necking or petting—or more. In extreme cases, according to Reik, sex is utterly selfish, using the object only to get satisfaction. If a man's interest in a woman is just sex, then when he is through having sex with her, he is through with her, period—until he gets the urge to have sex again.

By contrast, Reik thinks that "in no case can love be only selfish, or as selfish as sex. . . . It is always concerned with the welfare or happiness of the other person, regrets the other's absence [even right *after* sex], wants to be together with the object, feels lonely without it."[1]

## Signs of Love

If it is love, *your ego response tends to be unselfish and outgoing*. You care as much about what's good for the other as for yourself. You want her or him to get as much out of the relationship as you get. Love "is a state in which each one of two people realizes that his [or her] happiness can be attained only when the other also is happy. As a consequence, each one lives not only for [one's] self but for the other, sometimes even more for the other than for [one's] self."[2]

If you're in love, you will share thoughts, feelings, attitudes, plans, hopes, interests, even intimate things you would share with few if any others. And the more you share, the more committed to each other you will become. If you are in love, you will also want to keep these shared secrets pretty private—even sacred. You will want to keep your physical expressions of affection quite private. You will shy away from obvious necking and petting in public. It is no accident that those who display a lot of affection in public also tend to get low scores on emotional maturity tests.

## Commitment—a Law of Life

Not only is the unselfish commitment of one's self essential to a happy marriage. It is also important if we are to gain fullness of life in any area. One of the basic secrets of life is that a higher fulfillment of self comes as a result of committing one's self to something higher and greater than the self.

That's a lesson that the so-called "me" generation needs to learn. Such a commitment helps us to rise above mere concern with our own selfish needs and wants. It opens whole new horizons of value and meaning for our lives. The person least concerned about self is the person who becomes most fulfilled. This paradox was set forth by Jesus of Nazareth: "Whoever tries to keep his life will lose it, and whoever loses his life will preserve it."[3]

If you love a spouse or a family not for themselves, but because they are *your* spouse and *your* children, then that is selfish—another kind of self-love. This, like any other type of self-love, serves to keep you from finding your peak of fulfillment. So if you are to be fully mature, your circle of concern needs to reach out beyond the self, even beyond your own family and local community as well. Indeed, now our loving concern must include all people everywhere—the whole of planet earth.

To love another means that you wish to protect him or her from all harm. Since, as we have said, some threats to life are global—pollution, nuclear war or accident, ozone depletion, population growth—so must your concern be worldwide. We need to be citizens of the world. As George Wald once said, our concern must be with not only *what kind* of a future we will have, but *whether* we have a future at all. Each of us must now work to preserve that future, not only for ourselves, but for the ones we love and for all humankind. By so doing, we will get Life—with a capital "L."

# ... **19** ........

## CLUE THIRTEEN:
## What Is Your
## Overall Attitude?

*C* LOSELY related to your ego response is your general attitude toward your partner. Are you concerned solely with what you get out of the relationship? Or do you find yourself wanting to make sure the other person is happy, and that his or her needs are also being met?

### Signs of Infatuation

If you are infatuated, *your overall attitude is one of taking from the relationship*. You will find that your main concern is what *you* are getting out of it, plus what you hope to get in the future. The other person is seen as a means to gratify your own personal needs and wants, to attain your own goals and satisfactions.

You like the person *not* for what he or she is as a person, but for what that person does for you. You use the person as a stepping-stone to get things you want. Your partner helps you get attention, go places you like, satisfy your sex urge, climb the social ladder, get out of a bad home life, or a host of other private ends. In short, you exploit the other. If your main concern is to "look out for Number 1"—namely yourself—then look out. You are infatuated.

Such an attitude will not help you build a long, happy relationship. If you are willing to use the person for your own advantage before you marry, you will no doubt do so afterward as well. You will marry not for love, but for self-centered reasons such as greed or lust, position or prestige, a life of ease or security. These are scarcely the elements of real love. They grow instead out of selfishness and pride, which are in turn rooted in your ego response to the other person.

## Signs of Love

If you have found real love, you more and more want to give to, not take from, the other person and the relationship. *You want to share, give of yourself to your beloved.* You are intent on doing all you can to bring happiness to the other just as long as it does not spoil chances for his or her *future* fulfillment, or threaten your future together.

In years past it was the custom for the man to propose to his beloved on bended knee. "I want to spend my life making you happy," he would say. If he really meant that, if he was honestly longing to give of himself to bring fulfillment to his sweetheart, he was truly in love. When you are in love, you want your beloved to be as happy as you are. Your concern for that person and his or her welfare is at the very least on a par with concern for yourself. The beloved has come to be a part of you. You cannot be truly happy unless that person is happy, too. If you haven't yet reached that stage, then you probably do not love.

When you do reach this level of love, it may inspire a similar love in your beloved. Theodor Reik tells of the courtship of Moses Mendelssohn, the philosopher with a deformed body. Born small of stature and a hunchback, he fell in love with the daughter of a rich nobleman. She was so repelled by his looks that he had no chance to reveal to her his true self.

One day as he was leaving the city, he asked to bid her farewell.

> He found her busy with some needlework. She avoided looking at him during their conversation. Cleverly he led her around to the subject which was in his mind. She asked him whether he too believed that marriages are made in Heaven. "Certainly," he replied, "and something quite unusual happened to me. As you know, they call out in Heaven at the birth of a child, 'This one and that one will get this and that girl for a wife.' When I was born, my future wife was also thus announced, but it was added: 'She will, alas, have a terrible hump.' I shouted: 'Oh, God, Lord, a girl who is humpbacked will very easily become bitter and hard. A girl should be beautiful. Good Lord, give the hump to me and let her be handsome and well formed.' " The girl, deeply moved, stretched out her hand for Mendelssohn's. She became his faithful and loving wife.[1]

His tale of self-giving love, which conveyed the point that his own love was of like kind, helped her to look beyond his body and see his real self. She could tell that he knew what true love is all about. As Robert Blood says:

> It involves concern for the partner, interest in his [her] welfare, and effort to meet his [her] needs. Caring is intensely personal. The ministry of care is carried on joyously. He who truly cares never considers himself a martyr or deserving of special praise.[2]

Love is not used up in the giving. The more of it you give away, the more of it you have. Like a mountain spring, the supply seems endless.

Along with the receiver of love, the giver of love gets joyous rewards. The one who gives feels needed and useful. Some people say that all love is selfish. Since the one who loves and gives of self will in return get the reward of feeling useful, they claim, then that is also selfish. They see every human relationship as a selfish exchange, a give and take in the human marketplace. There is some truth in that view. Each of us does have needs, and we do seek to fill them.

But to assume that all love is selfish is to miss the main point of that paradox Jesus described. It is to confuse the intent of an act with the results of that act. "Whoever tries to save his own life will lose it." If you set out to save *your* life, that's a selfish *intent*. The *result* is that you lose out on life. You miss the joy of giving, of being useful, of feeling needed.

"Whoever loses his life will save it." The intent here is to lose (or forego) selfish self-fulfillment. And if you do that, what is the result? You actually get more of life. Why? Because you not only share the joys of the other person, but you also get lots of extra unsought joys as well—the joys of being useful and feeling needed.

## Putting a Finger on a Rule of Thumb

Teenagers sometimes ask me, "Can't you give us one simple rule we can use to tell whether it's love?" In one sense, no one rule can be enough. Each of the 14 clues is very important or it wouldn't be in the list at all. Each should be fully considered. But if I were forced to come up with just one key clue to help you determine whether you truly love, here's what it would be. It will separate the men from the boys and the women from the girls pretty fast.

*If you love someone so much that you want that person to be happy, even if you are not the one to make him or her happy, then you really love that person.* That is, if you love someone so much that you want that person to be happy, even if you can't be the one who *shares* that happiness, then your love is indeed real.

It is natural that, if you love a person, you long to be near, to share all life with that person. But if you love him or her enough, you'll want that person to be happy, whether or not you get to share in it.

If you are old enough and mature enough to marry, and if you find someone who loves you like that—and you feel the same way in return—think a long, long time before you let him or her get away. There aren't many loves like that around. If you find one, hang on to it if you can.

In most cases, of course, such love need not be denied. The couple will spend their lives together, devoted to the joy of making each other happy.

But what if you come to feel that you are not good for your beloved? Is your love so deep, is your desire for that person's happiness so great, that you are willing to give him or her up if you think it is best? That is the acid test of love.

But be sure you have read the signs right before you give up such a love. One young woman made a bad mistake.

Pam dearly loved a young man who was going into the ministry. But she had been divorced—and she knew that his church strongly opposed divorce. She concluded that if she were to marry him, it would spoil his life work. So she swallowed her own deep desire to marry him and gave him no encouragement when he tried to court her. He therefore thought she didn't love him, so they drifted apart.

His church later became much less rigid on the matter of divorce, and he eventually married a divorced woman. Pam remarried, but after many years she still loved that young minister. She had loved him enough to give him up, only to find that she had misread his needs and her ability to fill them. It is a bitter memory for them both. So proceed with care if you're considering giving up a true love.

# ... **20** .......

## CLUE FOURTEEN: Are You Jealous?

$\mathcal{J}$ EALOUSY may be a cultural universal—found everywhere. It pops up in all kinds of patterns and places. A new dad resents mom's time with the baby. Sister slugs the second child. Siblings become rivals. Spouses and sweethearts grow jealous if their beloveds show the slightest sign of fondness toward a rival—real or imagined.

Anthropologists find jealousy near and far. No society seems to be without it, even those in which more than one spouse is the accepted rule, and those where adultery is fully permitted.[1]

Even those with "open" marriages or live-in arrangements do not escape the green-eyed monster.[2] "True, there may very well be people who are secure enough within themselves not to be threatened by their spouse's openly having a sex relationship with another person," observes James McCary. "But, as Gracie Allen used to say, 'There are a lot of people like that, but not many.' "[3] Very few relationships survive if one party finds out the other has "cheated" on them. That almost always leads to intense jealousy, distrust, and rupture.[4]

Even Nena O'Neill, formerly an ardent advocate of sexually open marriages in her book, has changed her mind. She's found that open marriage has not worked for couples who have tried it, due to jealousy. She now advocates "one sexual partner for the rest of your life."[5]

So you too may well feel jealous, whether you're in love or infatuated, if the "object of your affection" shows even the slightest romantic interest in someone else. Jealousy will be especially strong if the couple is having sex with each other.

## Why Are We Jealous?

Some authorities say jealousy is a sign that we are insecure and unsure of ourselves; we have a "low self-image."[6] Others believe the roots of jealousy go back to childhood dependency when we tried to lay exclusive claim to our mother's love and care. Some think that groups of two persons lend themselves to a jealous desire to hold on to each other. "The sensitive union of two is always irritated by the spectator," even if the persons are mature and secure.[7]

Whatever its cause, the green-eyed monster provides us with the last clue to unlock the puzzle of love and infatuation. This clue is saved for last, not because jealousy is so important in itself. It is not. But its function can best be understood in the light of the two clues that precede it—ego response and overall attitude.

## Signs of Infatuation

Some people think jealousy is a true measure of love. They assume that the more jealous you are, the more you love your sweetheart. A young woman once said, "Oh,

Prof, he must love me so very much. If I even look at another boy, he blows his stack. He's so jealous he gets purplish green with rage." Is that real love? It clearly is not.

*It is in infatuation, not love, that jealousy is more frequent and more severe.* When you're jealous you want to fence in the other person, to keep him or her wholly to yourself. You are, in short, being selfish and possessive. Your concern is with what *you* want, not with what the *other person* wants. You're afraid that he or she might enjoy—or give some attention to—someone other than yourself.

Such a response is selfish. Your attitude is one of *taking* from your relationship. You are not willing to release the other person to do freely what he or she finds enjoyable. In effect, you are saying: "I want you to be happy, but only if you do what makes *me* happy. My happiness comes first, not yours." That is a sign of infatuation, not love.

Since marriages based on infatuation are much more likely to fail, it comes as no surprise that jealousy is strongly associated with divorce. More than three times as many divorced than happily married persons report mate jealousy.[8]

So jealousy is not a good sign—it is a danger signal. It does not cement a love relationship, it breaks it apart. The more jealousy there is, the more likely it is that you're infatuated.

## Signs of Love

*If it is love, jealousy is less frequent and less severe.* Not that you will never feel jealous. None of us ever gets to be 100% selfless. But the more you love the other person, the more you are able to release her or him. "Release is an expression of trust, respect, and acceptance."[9] To the extent that your love is not selfish, you can be free of jealousy.

If she likes to talk to another boy once in a while, he will not restrain her freedom. He wants her to be happy, even though he might prefer that she talk only with him all the time. She will not mind if he on occasion likes to dance with some other girl. Love does not restrict, it releases. It does not imprison, it liberates.

That's why it's so important that love be mutual. If you love, you trust. That means you need someone worthy of that trust. That way you can free each other to be your true selves, in full confidence that your trust will not be betrayed.

## Slaying the Green-Eyed Monster

But isn't it all right to try to make your beloved jealous once in a while, just so he or she will pay more attention to you? Not if you love him or her. That kind of pressure tactic is selfish. Love never tries to hurt the beloved.

In one sense, if members of the opposite sex are attracted to your beloved, it is a compliment to you. After all, who wants to admit to choosing someone so dull and unattractive that no other person would find him or her interesting? That your beloved is worthy of the notice of others is something to be proud of, not a cause for misery and fear.

As your love grows, so does your trust and confidence. More and more you learn to avoid the things that displease each other. As a result, jealousy comes to be less frequent and less severe. At length it may all but disappear.

# ... **21** ........

# Putting It
# All Together

$W$ E can now put all 14 clues together and construct a useful tool to describe the kind of love that will support a marriage.

Remember that no one clue alone—or even several—tells you enough to judge the true nature of a relationship. Instead, see how your romance stacks up with regard to the entire 14.

You must be utterly honest with yourself to get a sound, accurate reading. If you want it to come out "love" bad enough, you might drag the answers kicking and screaming into the love column, whether they belong there or not. If you cheat, you only cheat yourself. But if you use the clues with care and good judgment, they really will help you make the right choice.

### The Love/Infatuation Chart

The chart on pages 186-187 can help you make an accurate tally of how your romance scores on the love/infatuation continuum. After reading the 14 clues, you

# 14 KEY CLUES TO DISTINGUISH INFATUATION AND LOVE

| CLUES | CHARACTERISTICS | |
|---|---|---|
| **Questions to Ask** | **If It's Romantic Infatuation** | **If It's Real Love** |
| | **The nature of the attraction** | |
| 1. What is your main interest? What attracts you most? | Person's "physical equipment"; the body; what responds to the five senses. | The total personality; whole person; what's *in* the body. |
| 2. How many things attract you? | Few—though some may be very strong. | Many or most. |
| | **The course of the romance** | |
| 3. How did the romance start? | Fast (hours or days). | Slowly (months or years). |
| 4. How consistent is your level of interest? | Interest varies, comes and goes; many peaks and valleys; not consistent or predictable. | Evens out; gets to be dependable, consistent; can predict it. |
| 5. What effect does the romance have on your personality? | Disorganizing, destructive; you act strangely, are not "yourself." | Organizing, constructive; you're a better person. |
| 6. How does it end? | Fast—*unless* there's been mutually satisfying sex. | Slowly; takes long time; you may never be quite the same. |
| | **Two views of you two** | |
| 7. How do you view each other? | You live in a one-person world. You see the other as faultless, idealizing him or her. | You add the new relationship to former ones. You are more realistic, admitting other's faults, but loving anyway. |

|  | | |
|---|---|---|
| 8. How do others view you two? What's the attitude of friends and parents? | Few or none approve of the relationship. | Most or all approve. You get along well with other's friends and parents. |
| **Dealing with double trouble** | | |
| 9. What does distance (long separation) do to the relationship? | Withers away, dies; can't stand this added stress. | Survives; may even grow. |
| 10. How do quarrels affect the romance? | They get more frequent, more severe, and will kill relationship. | They grow less frequent, less severe. |
| **The inner world of love** | | |
| 11. How do you feel about and refer to your relationship? | Much use of I/me/my; he/him/his; she/her/hers; little feeling of oneness. | Speak of we/us/our; feel and think as a unit, a pair; togetherness. |
| 12. What's your ego response to the other? | Mainly selfish, restrictive; "What does this do for *me?*" | Mainly unselfish, releasing; concerned equally for other. |
| 13. What's your overall attitude toward the other? | Attitude of taking; exploit and use the other. | Attitude of giving, sharing; want to serve other's needs, wants. |
| 14. What is the effect of jealousy? | More frequent, more severe. | Less frequent, less severe. |
| TOTAL PATTERN OF THE CLUES | Kid stuff; romantic infatuation | The real thing; true love. |

Summary clue: In real love you love the person so much that you want them to be happy—even if you may not be allowed to share their happiness.

probably have a general impression of whether you're really in love. But to make such a great decision, you need a more accurate assessment.

Examine each clue with studied care. Give it a good deal of thought. Take all the time you need.

You want to find out not only *whether* a clue indicates you're in love, but also the *degree* to which it does that. You want to detect shades of difference in each of your ratings. To do that simply rate each clue on a scale of zero to ten. Zero stands for complete infatuation, ten for pure love.

| 0 | 1 | 2 | 3 | 4 | 5 | 6 | 7 | 8 | 9 | 10 |
|---|---|---|---|---|---|---|---|---|---|---|
| Infatuation | | | | | About even | | | | Love | |

Give each clue careful thought to see how it applies in your case. Think of as many aspects of the clue as you can, and the ways they affect you and your partner. Then choose the number on the scale which, by your soundest judgment, seems the most accurate description of your situation.

Take, for example, Clue 8: Do friends and parents approve? Suppose that you and your partner each have three close friends, and your parents are all living. If all but two of these ten friends and parents approve, your score would be eight. If only your mother and two of your sweetheart's friends approve, you score three. If none approves, you get a goose egg!

Unless you're rating a past romance, only 13 of the clues will apply. You can't tell how it will end if it hasn't ended yet, so Clue 6 cannot be rated. This means that a perfect love score for a current romance is 130 points—ten points each for 13 clues.

When you have rated your romance on all of the clues, add up all the numbers to get your total score.

## What Your Scores Mean

The higher your score is, of course, the more likely it is that you have real love. If you score 90 or above, that suggests a pretty solid love relationship. You can be encouraged. Your love is likely strong enough to support a successful marriage. There are two exceptions: (1) You may still be too young to marry. Or (2) you have not yet passed the test of time—a minimum of two full years of knowing each other well, but without being involved in a mutually satisfying sex life together.

In any case, you will still want to "make haste slowly" and take whatever precautions you feel might be needed.

Scores between 50 and 90 points would indicate a toss-up between love and pseudo-love. Your relationship shows some promise. Take more time to see which direction it goes. It may in time grow into love. Retest it from time to time.

If your score is less than 50, you are infatuated. Love is a very long way off. So take special care not to commit yourself very much to the relationship. Make no promises or plans for the future. Be sure that reason rules emotion—and don't let yourself get heavily involved in sex. Love may grow in time. You can, from time to time, rate your romance again to see if you detect any change. But above all, don't rush into anything.

### Meaning of Scores

| Score | Likely meaning | Action suggested |
|---|---|---|
| 0–50 | Infatuation | No promises or plans; don't commit yourself |
| 50–90 | Toss-up | Some hope; give it more time |

| 90–130 | Real love | Ponder marriage— with due care |
|--------|-----------|--------------------------------|

## So Now You Know

Your score should give you a general idea of the nature of your romance. The next question is: What should you do about it? Based on what you've learned, what kind of future does your romance probably have? It may help if we contrast the expected life spans of infatuation and love on a graph.

**General Life Spans of Infatuation and Love Compared**

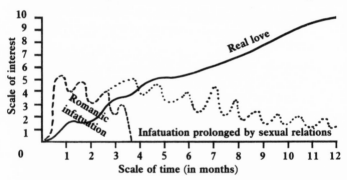

The chart above does not reflect the fine details of a particular romance. Its purpose is to provide a general picture of typical romances.

As we have seen, infatuation starts fast. Then the level of interest in the romance comes and goes, with lots of peaks and valleys. If the couple steers clear of heavy sex, infatuation does not last long. It grinds to a rather abrupt halt, unless real love emerges in the meantime.

If the couple allows a sex life to develop and both find it satisfying, interest in sex may keep the romance going for many months—even up to four or five years. But it will end in due time. Meanwhile, the couple's interest will continue to blow hot and cold. The grave danger is that the couple involved in sex likely won't be able to tell whether it's real love or just interest in sex that is holding them together—unless they arrange to be apart for a few months to test it out without the sex.

Love starts more slowly and grows as time goes by. The rough spots in the couple's early relationship slowly even out. Their interest keeps growing to a high level that they can maintain for years—even a lifetime. They come to count on their relationship being stable, secure, and satisfying.

## The Romance Risk

It should now be quite clear why "romantic love"—infatuation—is such a dangerous myth. If you marry on the strength of it, you take a terrible risk. Even if you add sex thrills to the infatuation equation, there is bound to be trouble ahead. Sex just prolongs the agony a little longer.

Granted, some couples may luck out. By chance their personalities may in the long run grow to be compatible. They may have the basic elements that can later build into real love.

But why gamble? What if it turns out that they do not have the potential for love between them? Their marriage may well be doomed at the outset. Based as it is on romance alone, it will likely falter, fade, and finally fail.

Romantic infatuation, the state most people call "love," is pseudo-love, a cheap substitute for the real thing. It lures its innocent victims to the altar, then dashes their lovely hopes in the marital mud.

Does all this mean you should shun all romantic infatuations? Are they all bad? Must you deny yourself all
those nice, warm, romantic feelings and pleasures? Not
at all.

## Infatuations Are Fine, *But* . . .

A good, lively infatuation can be a grand and glorious
thing. It can lift you to the clouds and open whole new
horizons. It can help you tap deep feelings and tender
emotions that you never dreamed you could have. This
is an emotional trip that each of us should take at least
once in life.

So when it hits you, don't fight it. Relax. Let it sweep
over you like a warm wave at the bathing beach. Just be
sure you don't let that wave of emotion drown your good
sense. And most important of all, *don't do anything drastic
about it right away.* Don't do anything foolish. By that we
mean two things.

First, be sure you don't get swept into some "quickie
commitment" that you might later regret. By all means,
take lots of time. Remind yourself that if the real stuff of
love is to be found in your relationship, it will still be
there next week and next month—and next year. No need
to hurry into anything. You can never go wrong by taking
your time. If your love is real, it will not fade. You can
afford to be cautious, to wait. Be slow even to label it
love. Above all, remind yourself that infatuation is never
enough to build a marriage on.

Second, don't be too quick to get involved in sex. You
will no doubt want very much to have sex. That is quite
normal. The urge may at times seem too strong to curb.
But sex can lead to a whole flock of new and needless
complications. It can dull your ability to think straight
about your relationship.

So wait for sex until after you have a firm grip on your feelings. Wait until you are quite sure that you really care about each other in a very dear way before you let much sex get into the act. And whatever you do, *don't flunk the test of time*.

## Infatuation May Grow into Love

If you determine that you're infatuated, not in love, you don't have to rush to end the relationship. Infatuation can and sometimes does develop into real love. If you sever a relationship the instant you realize it is—at that point—only infatuation, how will you ever know whether it would have grown into real love? Assume a wait-and-see attitude. If it doesn't last, fine. You have made no rash commitments, and you haven't dashed into sex, so you need have no regrets. If and when the break does come, you can much more easily accept it.

## Breaking It Up

After you've given a relationship a fair trial and you're convinced that it's an infatuation with no future, you may want to call it quits. If you decide to do that, of course, try not to hurt your partner any more than you have to. In some cases Cupid's wounds cut mighty deep. Remove the arrow with great care. Be as nice about it as you can.

At the same time, you do the person no favor by putting off the breakup. That is cruel. As soon as you are sure of your decision, tell him or her right away. It may not come as much of a surprise. You have probably dropped some strong hints along the way that you had your doubts about the relationship.

In any case, *be perfectly honest—and gently firm.* If you see no future at all in the situation, make that quite clear. If there is no hope, offer the person none. And explain in full your reasons for the break. Remain friends if you care to. But be firm in your decision before you act, then stick by it if you feel you are right. Remember, if it's infatuation for both of you, you will both tend to get over it fairly fast.

If the person threatens you in anger, stall until you can get protective support from parents or friends. If he or she tries to hold on to you by threatening self-harm or even suicide, that is a bluff—unless the person is mentally sick. Even so, you cannot be held responsible for the immature reactions of others if you've done your best to be kind and considerate, yet truthful. A relationship that is continued under the pressure of threat is no relationship at all.

## It's Time to Stop Snickering

All of this is fine for the person who has found real love, or who is infatuated and knows it. But what if you have a friend who is in the throes of an infatuation and *thinks* it's love? Should you just ignore it and hope the person comes to his or her senses? Should you just not talk about it for fear of losing your good relationship with that person? That is the strong temptation, but is it right?

Some people just laugh it off. We have a curious quirk in our culture. We are amused when others are in discomfort or danger. We giggle at the guy who whacks his thumb with a hammer or the girl who has ripped an embarrassing hole in her swimsuit. We guffaw at the pitiful drunk when his coordination has been impaired by booze. We snicker at the youngster—or oldster—who is so smitten with romantic infatuation that he or she behaves like a fool.

Why should we laugh at the antics of one who has crippled both body and mind with alcohol or other drugs? And why are we amused when persons become infatuated, lose their appetites, and do strange things? Or worse still, when they move quickly into marriage, even though the two of them have little or nothing in common?

Instead of laughing at an infatuated friend, maybe you ought to cry, or at least cry out—in solemn warning. What if you saw that same friend skiing rapidly downhill toward an unseen rock? If you knew—as we know with marriage—that the chances of tragedy were 50-50, would you laugh? Would you say without concern: "Well, it's Peg's life—if she wrecks it that's her business"? No! You'd yell: "Hey! Look out for that rock!" Getting into a miserable marriage is far from funny. Maybe our first step toward a remedy is to stop laughing. Why not start talking sense to the persons involved?

## Full Freedom—to Fail?

We live in one of the few places on this whole planet where youths are allowed full freedom to choose their own mates. In most cultures marriage is considered far too important to be left to the inexperienced and immature young. The choice of partners is made by the families or matchmakers. The decision is based on reason, not romance. If love develops at all, it comes after the marriage, not before. Most cultures see "romantic love" as a condition that is "here today but gone tomorrow." Hence it is thought to be far too frail a foundation for marriage. And they are right. Such a system may seem strange to us, but these cultures have very few marriages that fail.

In the best arranged marriages, care is taken that the couple will be compatible, that they are a good match. This assures that the couple will have lots of things in common. It gives them a firm base for getting along well. Of course, it has an obvious defect. It robs the couple of their own free choice. They have to take what they get. But love almost always does come.

On the other hand, marriages based on romance, such as those in America, allow people full freedom to choose their own mates. Once they are of age, they are free to act on their own best judgment. They can—and often do—ignore the wishes of families, friends, and everyone else. That's a big mistake.

A couple may pay a high price for that freedom. "Romantic love" (infatuation) doesn't last long. It's flimsy and fickle. Then, too, the couple's eyes are often so full of stars that they fail to see the true nature of each other. Their pink cloud is often shrouded in fog. They may skip over many important facts that ought to be considered in their decision. The chances for their mating success are therefore much reduced.

Now, I do not suggest a return to the arranged marriage. That would never catch on in our freedom-loving Western world. But I do think there's a better way to choose mates. We can preserve the best values from both systems of mate choice, and at the same time avoid their risks.

## How to Have Your Wedding Cake and Eat It Too

How can you have the best of both worlds? For one thing, you can be careful to match up the main factors in your own personality and background with those of a likely mate. Give it careful thought. Then you can ask the honest opinion of your family and friends about the person you think might be a good choice—and *listen with great care to what they say.* You can make use of test scores and computer results. You can master the 14 clues and become expert in the art of using them. You can thereby see what social science has already found out about how to tell real love from romantic fool's gold.

If you do these things well, you can have your wedding cake and eat it too. You can preserve your right to choose, yet glean most of the benefits of the more stable arranged marriage. In brief, you can apply realism and good sense to your problem.

## Two + *Tu* + True = One

This may sound like terrible math, but it's actually a good formula for sound mate choice.

The French have two words that mean "you"—*vous* and *tu*. They use *vous* when they speak to someone they don't know very well. They use *tu* if the person is a beloved friend or relative.

So here's the proper "recipe" for a good marriage. Take *two* normal, mature persons. Add a close *"tu"* relationship (with or without romantic infatuation). Let slowly simmer in strong solution of careful consulting with friends and families. Add common interests. Then stir in generous helpings of their own good sense, and chill with the *true* findings of science. Mix the ingredients well. This will produce a happy, lasting union with strong bonds.

If followed with due care, this formula could bring a dramatic change in the rates of marital failure in every society where romance is now the main basis for mating. This is a recipe you can bet your life on.

And when it comes right down to it, that's exactly what you're doing when you wed—you're betting your life.

Some of the words in those wedding vows will read: " 'til death do us part." That's a pretty long time! You'll want to make doubly sure you don't mess up when you choose that life mate.

## The Sacred Right to Cocreate

One of the great privileges of marriage is to have children. It is indeed a sacred right. Did you ever take a close look at a newborn baby? So tiny, so fragile, so precious, so full of promise for the future. Tagore, the Indian poet, once said that every time a baby is born it is a sign that God has not yet lost hope for this world. It is indeed a miracle of miracles.

And just think: you and the one you come to love can claim the right to help cocreate another little human being! What a sacred trust! What a joy when that tiny babe comes as a gift from God, with the full blessing of society and your loved ones.

But how sobering to think: those two little eyes would never have opened if you two had not been intimate. Those tiny fingers and hands would never have touched if you had not shared with each other. That little mind would never have thought and reasoned and willed without the love of you and your mate.

What a responsibility! No wonder my old teacher Hornell Hart used to furrow his brow at us and exclaim: "How dare you look upon sex as just a plaything!"

How dare we, indeed! In a time when we are rediscovering and stressing the joys and pleasures of sex, there is grave danger that we will fail to grasp the deeper meaning of sex—the sacred right to cocreate. *Sex is a joy, but it's not a toy.* It is a high privilege, not to be taken lightly. It should be an act of loving, of real caring and sharing.

In its fullest meaning, sex is a sacred ritual through which two human persons are joined in every part of their being.

I hope you find that kind of sharing. Don't settle for anything less.

Have a rich love—and a happy life.

# Appendix: About AIDS

*A* number of reasons make this section necessary. First, AIDS is fatal, currently has no cure, and is spreading rapidly. Second, many people, especially those in their teens, don't know the basics about AIDS.[1] Third, teens are at higher risk than most of contracting AIDS because they are far less likely to avoid the chances of getting it.

This section provides a convenient summary of facts currently known about AIDS. True, more and more people are getting better informed about this deadly disease. Former U. S. Surgeon General C. Everett Koop sent an eight-page flyer to every mailing address in the U. S. in 1988.[2] However, studies showed that a large share did not read it. Fewer still discussed it with another. That could be a tragic error.

Many of us think the AIDS virus may spread faster among teens in the 1990s than among any other group. For example, most sexually active teens who use condoms—or any other birth-control method—have higher rates of contraceptive failure than older users.[3] That does not bode well for the future.

In preparing the surgeon general's eight-page flyer, some of the top health experts in the U. S. were consulted. It is a fine, readable survey and has, for the most part, been reprinted here. Some editing of the flyer's text has been necessary for use in this book. These edits are enclosed in brackets. Here are some things you should know about AIDS:

## What AIDS Means to You

AIDS is one of the most serious health problems that has ever faced the American public. It is important that we all, regardless of who we are, understand this disease.

AIDS stands for *acquired immunodeficiency syndrome*. It is a disease caused by the Human Immunodeficiency Virus, HIV—the AIDS virus.

The AIDS virus may live in the human body for years before actual symptoms appear. It primarily affects you by making you unable to fight other diseases. These other diseases can kill you.

Many people feel that only certain "high risk groups" of people are infected by the AIDS virus. This is untrue. [Men, women, children, babies—anyone can get AIDS.] *Who you are has nothing to do with whether you are in danger of being infected with the AIDS virus. What matters is what you do.*

People are worried about getting AIDS. Some should be worried and need to take some serious precautions. But many are not in danger of contracting AIDS.

The purpose of this [appendix] is to tell you how you can, and just as important, how you can't become infected with the AIDS virus.

Children need to know about AIDS. Discuss it with them as you would any health concern.

## How Do You Get AIDS?

There are two main ways you can get AIDS. First, you can become infected by having sex—oral, anal or vaginal—with someone who is infected with the AIDS virus.

Second, you can be infected by sharing drug needles and syringes with an infected person.

Babies of women who have been infected with the AIDS virus may be born with the infection because it can be transmitted from the mother to the baby before or during birth.

In addition, some persons with hemophilia and others have been infected by receiving blood.

### *The difference between giving and receiving blood*

**1. Giving blood.** You are not now, nor have you ever been in danger of getting AIDS from giving blood at a blood bank. The needles that are used for blood donations are brand-new. Once they are used, they are destroyed. There is no way you can come into contact with the AIDS virus by donating blood.

**2. Receiving blood.** The risk of getting AIDS from a blood transfusion has been greatly reduced. In the interest of making the blood supply as safe as possible, donors are screened for risk factors and donated blood is tested for the AIDS antibody. Call your local blood bank if you have questions.

## How Do You Get AIDS from Sex?

The AIDS virus can be spread by sexual intercourse whether you are male or female, heterosexual, bisexual or homosexual.

This happens because a person infected with the AIDS virus may have the virus in semen or vaginal fluids. The virus can enter the body through the vagina, penis, rectum or mouth.

Anal intercourse, with or without a condom, is risky. The rectum is easily injured during anal intercourse.

Remember, AIDS is sexually transmitted, and the AIDS virus is not the only infection that is passed through intimate sexual contact.

Other sexually transmitted diseases, such as gonorrhea, syphilis, herpes and chlamydia, can also be contracted through oral, anal and vaginal intercourse. If you are infected with one of these diseases and engage in risky behavior (*see* [*below*]), you are at greater risk of getting AIDS.

## Can You Become Infected?

Yes, if you engage in risky behavior.

The male homosexual population was the first in this country to feel the effects of the disease. But in spite of what you may have heard, the number of heterosexual cases is growing.

People who have died of AIDS in the U.S. have been male and female, rich and poor, white, Black, Hispanic, Asian and American Indian.

## What Behavior Puts You at Risk?

You are at risk of being infected with the AIDS virus if you have sex with someone who is infected, or if you share drug needles and syringes with someone who is infected.

Since you can't be sure who is infected, your chances of coming into contact with the virus increase with the number of sex partners you have. Any exchange of infected blood, semen or vaginal fluids can spread the virus and place you at great risk.

*The following behaviors are risky when performed with an infected person. You can't tell by looking if a person is infected.*

### Risky Behavior

Sharing drug needles and syringes.

Anal sex, with or without a condom.

Vaginal or oral sex with someone who shoots drugs or engages in anal sex.

Sex with someone you don't know well (a pickup or prostitute) or with someone you know has several sex partners.

Unprotected sex (without a condom) with an infected person.

### Safe Behavior

Not having sex.

Sex with one mutually faithful, uninfected partner.

Not shooting drugs.

## You Won't Get AIDS from Insects—or a Kiss

No matter what you may have heard, the AIDS virus is hard to get and is easily avoided.

You won't just "catch" AIDS like a cold or flu because the virus is a different type. The AIDS virus is transmitted through sexual intercourse, the sharing of drug needles, or to babies of infected mothers before or during birth.

*You won't get the AIDS virus through everyday contact* with the people around you in school, in the workplace, at parties, child care centers, or stores. You won't get it by swimming in a pool, even if someone in the pool is infected with the AIDS virus. Students attending school with someone infected with the AIDS virus are not in danger from casual contact.

*You won't get AIDS from a mosquito bite.* The AIDS virus is not transmitted through a mosquito's salivary glands like other diseases such as malaria or yellow fever. You won't get it from bed bugs, lice, flies or other insects, either.

*You won't get AIDS from saliva, sweat, tears, urine or a bowel movement.*

*You won't get AIDS from a kiss.*

*You won't get AIDS from clothes, a telephone, or from a toilet seat.* It can't be passed by using a glass or eating utensils that someone else has used. You won't get the virus by being on a bus, train or crowded elevator with a person who is infected with the virus, or who has AIDS.

## What about Dating?

Dating and getting to know other people is a normal part of life. Dating doesn't mean the same thing as having sex. Sexual intercourse as a part of dating can be risky. One of the risks is AIDS.

How can you tell if someone you're dating or would like to date has been exposed to the AIDS virus? The bad news is, you can't. But the good news is, as long as sexual activity and sharing drug needles are avoided, it doesn't matter.

You are going to have to be careful about the person you become sexually involved with, making your own decision based on your own best judgment. That can be difficult.

Has this person had any sexually transmitted diseases? How many people have they been to bed with? Have they experimented with drugs? All these are sensitive, but important, questions. But you have a personal responsibility to ask.

Think of it this way. If you know someone well enough to have sex, then you should be able to talk about AIDS. If someone is unwilling to talk, you shouldn't have sex.

[Can you trust a person to tell the truth about whether they have AIDS or have been exposed to the virus? Don't count on it. Studies just published show that a rather large percentage of persons said they would lie about that in order to get sex.]

## Do Married People Get AIDS?

Married people who are uninfected, faithful and don't shoot drugs are not at risk. But if they engage in risky behavior (*see* [*above*]), they can become infected with the AIDS virus and infect their partners. If you feel your spouse may be putting you at risk, talk to him or her. It's your life.

[AIDS counselor Sally Jue has this bit of advice for parents:] "Talk to your teenagers about AIDS. It is primarily a sexually transmitted disease. So if you're going to talk about AIDS, there's no way you can avoid talking about sex."

## What Is All the Talk about Condoms?

Not so very long ago, condoms (rubbers or prophylactics) were things we didn't talk about very much.

Now, they're discussed on the evening news and on the front page of your newspaper, and displayed out in the open in your local drugstore, grocery, and convenience store.

For those who are sexually active and not limiting their sexual activity to one partner, condoms have been shown to help prevent the spread of sexually transmitted diseases. That is why the use of condoms is recommended to help reduce the spread of AIDS.

Condoms are the best preventive measure against AIDS besides not having sex and practicing safe behavior (*see* [*above*]).

But condoms are far from being foolproof. You have to use them properly. And you have to use them every time you have sex, from start to finish. If you use a condom, you should remember these guidelines:

(1) Use condoms made of latex rubber. Latex serves as a barrier to the virus. "Lambskin" or "natural membrane" condoms are not as good because of the pores in the material. Look for the word "latex" on the package.

(2) A condom with a spermicide may provide additional protection. Spermicides have been shown in laboratory tests to kill the virus. Use the spermicide in the tip and outside of the condom.

(3) Condom use is safer with a lubricant. Check the list of ingredients on the back of the lubricant package to make sure the lubricant is water-based. Do not use petroleum-based jelly, cold cream, baby oil or cooking shortening. These can weaken the condom and cause it to break.

[But remember. There is no such thing as "safe" sex. Research revealed that 20% of the condoms sold in the U.S.leak. Best to test a condom first by filling it with lots of water and watching for any leakage. *Condoms provide safer sex, but not safe sex.*]

## Is There a Cure for AIDS?

There is presently no cure for AIDS.

Medicines such as AZT have prolonged the lives of some people with AIDS. There is hope that additional treatments will be found.

There is also no vaccine to prevent uninfected people from getting the infection. Researchers believe it may take years for an effective, safe vaccine to be found.

The most effective way to prevent AIDS is avoiding exposure to the virus, which you can control by your own behavior.

## What Does Someone with AIDS Look Like?

[They probably look just like anyone else.]

"You can't tell if someone has been infected by the AIDS virus by looking at him or her. But you aren't in danger of getting the disease unless you engage in risky behavior with someone who is infected," [according to] Anthony S. Fauci, M.D., Director, National Institute of Allergy and Infectious Diseases and Coordinator of the National Institutes of Health AIDS Research.

It is very important that everyone understands that a person can be infected with the AIDS virus without showing any symptoms at all.

It is possible to be infected for years, feel fine, look fine and have no way of knowing you are infected unless you have a test for the AIDS virus.

During this period, however, people infected with the AIDS virus can pass the virus to sexual partners, to people with whom drug needles are shared, and to children before or during birth. That is one of the most disturbing things about AIDS.

Once symptoms do appear, they are similar to the symptoms of some other diseases. As the disease progresses, they become more serious. That is because the AIDS virus keeps your body's natural defenses from operating correctly.

If you are concerned whether you might be infected, consider your own behavior and its effects on others. If you feel you need to be tested for the AIDS virus, talk to a doctor or an AIDS counselor for more information.

## Should You Get an AIDS Test?

[Not unless you have put yourself at risk.]

You have probably heard about the "AIDS Test." The test doesn't actually tell you if you have AIDS. It shows if you have been infected with the virus. It looks for changes in blood that occur after you have been infected.

The Public Health Service recommends you be confidentially counseled and tested if you have had any sexually transmitted disease or shared needles; if you are a man who has had sex with another man; or if you have had sex with a prostitute, male or female. You should be tested if you have had sex with anyone who has done any of these things.

If you are a woman who has been engaging in risky behavior (*see* [*above*]), and you plan to have a baby or are not using birth control, you should be tested.

Your doctor may advise you to be counseled and tested if you are a hemophiliac, or have received a blood transfusion between 1978 and 1985.

If you test positive, and find you have been infected with the AIDS virus, you must take steps to protect your partner.

People who have always practiced safe behavior do not need to be tested.

There's been a great deal in the press about problems with the test. It is very reliable if it is done by a good laboratory and the results are checked by a physician or counselor.

If you have engaged in risky behavior, speak frankly to a doctor who understands the AIDS problem, or to an AIDS counselor.

For more information, call your local public health agency. They're listed in the government section of your phone book. Or, call your local AIDS hotline. If you can't find the number, call 1-800-342-AIDS.

## The Problem of Drugs and AIDS

Today, in some cities, the sharing of drug needles and syringes by those who shoot drugs is the fastest growing way that the virus is being spread.

No one should shoot drugs. It can result in addiction, poor health, family disruption, emotional disturbances and death. Many drug users are addicted and need to enter a drug treatment program as quickly as possible.

In the meantime, these people must avoid AIDS by not sharing any of the equipment used to prepare and inject illegal drugs.

Sharing drug needles, even once, is an extremely easy way to be infected with the AIDS virus. Blood from an infected person can be trapped in the needle or syringe, and then injected directly into the bloodstream of the next person who uses the needle.

Other kinds of drugs, including alcohol, can also cause problems. Under their influence, your judgment becomes impaired. You could be exposed to the AIDS virus while doing things you wouldn't otherwise do.

Teenagers are at an age when trying different things is especially inviting. They must understand how serious the drug problem is and how to avoid it.

Drugs are also one of the main ways in which prostitutes become infected. They may share needles themselves or have sex with people who do. They then can pass the AIDS virus to others.

For information about drug abuse treatment programs, contact your physician, local public health agency or community AIDS or drug assistance group.

## AIDS and Babies

An infected woman can give the AIDS virus to her baby before it is born, or during birth. If a woman is infected, her child has about one chance in two of being born with the virus.

If you are considering having a baby, and think you might have been at risk of being infected with the AIDS virus, even if it was years ago, you should receive counseling and be tested before you get pregnant.

You must have a long talk with the person with whom you're planning to have a child. Even if you have known this person for a long time, there's no way to be sure he or she hasn't been infected in the past, possibly without realizing it. That person needs to think hard and decide if an AIDS test might be a good idea. So should you.

Carmen Reyes has AIDS. [She says:] "I quit using drugs five years before my baby was born. I didn't know I was infected with AIDS until he was diagnosed. You have to find out."

## Talking with Kids about AIDS

Children hear about AIDS, just as we all do. But they don't understand it, so they become frightened. They are worried they or their friends might get sick and die.

Children need to be told they can't get AIDS from everyday contact in the classroom, cafeteria or bathrooms.

They don't have to worry about getting AIDS even if one of their schoolmates is infected.

Basic health education should be started as early as possible, in keeping with parental and community standards. Local schools have the responsibility to see that their students know the facts about AIDS. It is very important that middle school students—those entering their teens—learn to protect themselves from the AIDS virus.

Children must also be taught values and responsibility, as well as skills to help them resist peer pressure that might lead to risky behavior. These skills can be reinforced by religious and community groups. However, final responsibility rests with the parents. As a parent, you should read and discuss this [material] with your children.

## Helping a Person with AIDS

If you are one of the growing number of people who know someone who is infected, you need to have a special understanding of the problem.

No one will require more support and more love than your friend with AIDS. Feel free to offer what you can, without fear of becoming infected.

Don't worry about getting AIDS from everyday contact with a person with AIDS. You need to take precautions such as wearing rubber gloves only when blood is present.

If you don't know anyone with AIDS, but you'd still like to offer a helping hand, become a volunteer. You can be sure your help will be appreciated by a person with AIDS.

This might mean dropping by the supermarket to pick up groceries, sitting with the person a while, or just being there to talk. You may even want to enroll in a support group for caregivers. These are available around the country. If you are interested, contact any local AIDS-related organization.

Above all, keep an upbeat attitude. It will help you and everyone face the disease more comfortably.

## Want to Know More about AIDS?

James O. Mason, M.D., Director, Centers for Disease Control [suggests:] "If you want more information about AIDS or what you can do to help, contact your physician, community organizations in your area, or the local public health agency."

# Notes

**Chapter 1**

1. William M. Kephart, *The Family, Society and the Individual*, 3rd ed. (Boston: Houghton Mifflin, 1972), p. 349.
2. Paul Popenoe, "The Romantic Complex," *Family Life Magazine* (reprint).
3. 1 Corinthians 13:4-7.
4. William Proxmire, former senator from Wisconsin, press release dated March 11, 1975. See also reply by Ellen Berscheid, Professor of Psychology, University of Minnesota at Minneapolis, in John W. Kole, "Proxmire barb goes unloved," *Milwaukee Journal*, March 11, 1975, p. 4. She "said that Senator Proxmire was trying to turn back the clock by criticizing valid research about love. 'Sen. Proxmire himself has suffered marital separation. I would think that he especially would want to understand about love being the basis for the marriage contract.' Proxmire, [then] 59, announced last month that he and his wife, Ellen, had reached a reconciliation after more than 3½ years of separation."
5. Merton P. Strommen, *Five Cries of Youth* (New York: Harper and Row, 1974), p. 25.
6. Dianne Kieren, June Henton, and Rainona Marotz, *His and Hers: A Problem Solving Approach to Marriage* (Hinsdale,Ill.: The Dryden Press, 1975), p. 50.
7. Albert Ellis, "Love and family relationships of American college girls," *The American Journal of Sociology* 55 (May 1950): 554.
8. Kephart, *Family*, p. 347. For findings relative to that study, see William M. Kephart, "Some correlates of romantic love," *Journal*

*of Marriage and the Family* 29 (August 1967): 470–474; and "The 'Dysfunctional' Theory of romantic love: A research report," *Journal of Comparative Family Studies* 1 (Autumn 1970): 26–36.

9. Ernest W. Burgess, Paul Wallin, and Gladys Denny Schultz, *Courtship, Engagement and Marriage* (Philadelphia: Lippincott, 1954), p. 136.

10. Gilbert V. Hamilton, *A Research in Marriage* (New York: Albert and Charles Boni, 1929); Clifford Kirkpatrick and Theodor Caplow, "Emotional trends in the courtship experience of college students as expressed by graphs with some observations on methodological implications," *American Sociological Review* 10:5 (October 1945): 619.

11. Leonard Benson, *The Family Bond: Marriage, Love and Sex in America* (New York: Random House, 1971), p. 116.

12. Kephart, *Family*, p. 348.

13. Benson, *Family Bond*, p. 116.

14. D. G. Dean, "Romanticism and emotional maturity: A further exploration," *Social Forces* 42 (March 1964): 298–303. See also William L. Kolb, "Family sociology, marriage education, and the romantic complex," *Social Forces* 29 (October 1950): 65–72.

15. Andreas Capellanus, *The Art of Courtly Love*, abr. and ed., Frederick W. Locke (New York: Frederick Ungar Publishing Co., 1957), p. 4; also in William N. Stephens, ed., *Reflections on Marriage* (New York: Thomas Y. Crowell, 1968), p. 42.

## Chapter 2

1. Paul C. Glick, "Marriage, divorce, and living arrangements: Prospective changes," *Journal of Family Issues* 5 (March 1984): 9–11.

2. Raoul de Roussy de Sales, "Love in America," *Atlantic Monthly* 161 (May 1938): 645.

3. Ross Stagner, *Psychology of Personality*, 2nd ed. (New York: McGraw–Hill, 1948), p. 379.

4. Paul C. Glick and Sung–Ling Lin, "Recent changes in divorce and remarriage," *Journal of Marriage and the Family* 48 (November 1986): 739; and Steven L. Nock, "The family and hierarchy," *Journal of Marriage and the Family* 50 (November 1988): 960.

5. Glick, "Marriage, divorce," p. 7; and Alfred Demaris, "A comparison of remarriages with first marriages on satisfaction in marriage and its relationship to prior cohabitation," *Family Relations* 33 (July 1984): 443.

6. Glick and Lin, "Recent changes," pp. 737–738.

7. Ibid., p. 738; also Graham B. Spanier and P. C. Glick, "Marital instability in the United States: some correlates and recent changes," *Family Relations* 30 (July 1981): 329.
8. Glick, "Marriage, divorce," p. 7: "About one-half of the first marriages of young adults today are likely to end in divorce. For second marriages the projected level is 60%."
9. Charles E. Welch and Paul C. Glick, "International trends in marriage and divorce," *International Journal of Sociology of the Family* 12 (Spring 1982): 121. "The U.S. typically maintains the highest marriage and divorce rates in the world."
10. Judson T. and Mary G. Landis, *Building a Successful Marriage*, 7th ed. (Englewood Cliffs, N.J.: Prentice–Hall, 1977).
11. Lloyd Saxton, *The Individual, Marriage, and the Family*, 6th ed. (Belmont, Calif.: Wadsworth Publishing Co., 1986; see also Paul C. Glick, *American Families* (New York: John Wiley and Sons, 1957); Hugh Carter and Paul C. Glick, *Marriage and Divorce: A Social and Economic Study* (Cambridge, Mass.: Harvard University Press, 1970), pp. 38–39.
12. Alan E. Bayer, "Early dating and early marriage," *Journal of Marriage and the Family* 30 (November 1968): 631.
13. Douglas M. Teti, Michael E. Lamb, and Arthur B. Elster, "Long-range socioeconomic and marital consequences of adolescent marriage in three cohorts of adult males," *Journal of Marriage and the Family* 49 (August 1987): 499–506. Also D. M. Teti and M. E. Lamb, "Socioeconomic and marital outcomes of adolescent marriage, adolescent childbirth, and their co-occurrence," *Journal of Marriage and Family* 51 (February 1989): 204–212; and Alan Booth and John N. Edwards, "Age at marriage and marital instability," *Journal of Marriage and the Family* 47 (February 1985): 67–68.
14. William F. Pratt, "A Study of Marriages Involving Premarital Pregnancies," Dissertation, Department of Sociology, University of Michigan, 1965; also Teti and Lamb, "Socioeconomic," 1989, p. 203.
15. Horace Gary, "Courtship and conception," *Medical Times* 89 (July 1961): 677–680; also Teti, Lamb, and Elster, "Long-range socioeconomic," pp. 499–506.
16. Saxton, *Individual and Family*.
17. Teti and Lamb, "Socioeconomic," pp. 203ff.
18. Robert F. Winch, *The Modern Family*, rev. ed. (New York: Henry Holt, 1964). Also Saxton, *Individual and Family*.
19. "Too young," words by Sylvia Dee, music by Sid Lippman, Jefferson Music Co., 1951.

20. Burgess and Cottrell, *Predicting Success,* 1939. See also Landis and Landis, *Building Marriage,* pp. 6, 90–94; and Judson T. Landis, "The pattern of divorce in three generations," *Social Forces* 34:3 (March 1956): 213–216; and Juliette L. Despert, *Children of Divorce,* 1st ed. (Garden City, N.Y.: Doubleday, 1962), preface.

21. Verna M. Keith and Barbara Findley, "The impact of parental divorce on children's educational attainment, marital timing, and likelihood of divorce," *Journal of Marriage and the Family* 50 (August 1988): 797; also Bert N. Adams, "Fifty years of family research: what does it mean?" *Journal of Marriage and the Family* 50 (February 1988): 10; David H. Knox Jr. and Michael J. Sporakowski, "Attitudes of college students toward love," *Journal of Marriage and the Family* 30 (November 1968): 638–642. See also Benson, *Family Bond,* p. 116, and Kephart, "Some correlates," pp. 569–578.

22. Adams, "Fifty Years," p. 10.

23. Sexton, *Individual and Family.*

24. Nancy Moore Clatworthy, "Living together," in Nona Glazer-Malbin, *Old Family/New Family: Interpersonal Relationships* (New York: D. Van Nostrand Co., 1975), pp. 67–89.

25. Paul C. Glick and Graham B. Spanier, "Married and unmarried cohabitation in the United States," *Journal of Marriage and the Family* 42 (February 1980): 21; see also Richard R. Clayton and Harwin L. Voss, "Shacking up; Cohabitation in the 1970s," *Journal of Marriage and the Family* 39 (May 1977): 273–284.

26. Paul Popenoe and Donna Wicks, "Marital Happiness in Two Generations," *Mental Hygiene* 21 (April 1937): 218–233; and "Together: An alternative to marriage," *Journal of Marriage and the Family* 34 (May 1972): 305–312. See also Barbara Risman, Charles T. Hill, and others, "Living together in college: Implications for courtship," *Journal of Marriage and the Family* 43 (February 1981): 77–83.

27. Noel Myricks, " 'Palimony': The impact of Marvin v. Marvin," *Family Relations* 29 (April 1980): 210–215.

28. Ray E. Short, *Sex, Dating and Love: 77 Questions Most Often Asked.* (Minneapolis: Augsburg, 1984), "Is living-in flunking out?" pp. 88–112; also Roy E. L. Watson, "Premarital cohabitation vs. traditional courtship: Their effects on subsequent marital adjustment," *Family Relations* 32 (January 1983): 139–147; Alfred Demaris, "A comparison," 443–449; and Patricia A. Gwartney Gibbs, "The institutionalization of premarital cohabitation: Estimates from marriage license applications, 1970 and 1980," *Journal of Marriage and the Family* 48 (May 1986): 423–434; Eleanor D. Macklin, "Heterosexual cohabitation among unmarried college students," *Family Coordinator* (October 1972): 463–471.

**Chapter 3**

1. Denis de Rougemont, *Love in the Western World* (New York: Harcourt, Brace & Co., 1940), pp. 75–76.
2. Wendell Johnson, *People in Quandaries* (New York: Harper and Brothers, 1946), pp. 14–20.
3. William Graham Cole, *Sex and Love in the Bible* (New York: Association Press, 1959), p. 53.
4. C. S. Lewis, *The Four Loves* (New York: Harcourt, Brace & Co., 1971), p. 106.
5. Theodor Reik, *Of Love and Lust: On the Psychoanalysis of Romantic and Sexual Emotions* (New York: Farrar, Straus and Cudahy, 1957), especially Part 1.
6. Unpublished work by P. K. Houdek provides much of the basic framework for these 14 clues.

**Chapter 4**

1. Robert R. and P. L. Bell, "Sexual satisfaction among married women," *Medical Aspects of Human Sexuality* 6 (December 1972): 136–144. Also Alfred C. Kinsey and others, *Sexual Behavior in the Human Male* (Philadelphia: Saunders, 1948); and *Sexual Behavior in the Human Female* (Philadelphia: Saunders, 1953).
2. From studies reported at the national meeting of the American Association for the Advancement of Science, in New Orleans, reported in the *Milwaukee Journal*, February 19, 1990, pp. 1a, 8a. Research done in 1989 by the General Social Survey Group, University of Chicago.
3. From a second study reported at the AAAS conference, of 1,880 never-married males ages 15–19, interviewed in 1988 by Freya Sonenstein and others at the Urban Institute, Washington, D.C., reported in the *Milwaukee Journal*, February 19, 1990.
4. Luther G. Baker, "In my opinion: the sexual revolution in perspective," *Family Relations* 32 (April 1983): 297–300. Baker is a certified marital and sexual therapist.

**Chapter 5**

1. Landis and Landis, *Building Marriage*, pp. 166–167; see also Paul C. Glick, "Fifty years of family demography: A record of social change," *Journal of Marriage and the Family* 50 (November 1988): 861–873; also Morval D. Glenn and Michael Supanic, "The social

and demographic correlates of divorce and separation in the United States: An update and reconsideration," *Journal of Marriage and the Family* 46 (1984): 563–576.

2. Zick Rubin, *Liking and Loving: An Invitation to Social Psychology* (New York: Holt, Rinehart and Winston, 1973), p. 113.

**Chapter 7**

1. James Leslie McCary, *Freedom and Growth in Marriage* (Santa Barbara, Calif.: Hamilton Publishing Co., 1975), p. 137.

**Chapter 8**

1. Shirley Lord, "Conversation about being in love," *Harper's Bazaar* 103 (May 1970): 60.

2. Robert K. Kelly, *Courtship, Marriage, and the Family* (New York: Harcourt, Brace and World, Inc., 1969), p. 213.

3. Reik, *Of Love,* p. 80.

4. J. L. and Alma L. Hirning, *Marriage Adjustment* (New York: American Book Co., 1956), p. 123; Evelyn M. Duvall and Reuben Hill, *When You Marry,* rev. ed. (New York: Association Press, 1953), pp. 40–41, 43.

5. Duvall and Hill, *When You Marry,* p. 30.

6. Judson T. and Mary G. Landis, *Building a Successful Marriage,* 7th ed. (Englewood Cliffs, N.J.: Prentice-Hall, 1977), pp. 119–120.

**Chapter 10**

1. David L. Weis and Joan Jurich, "Size of community of residence as a predictor of attitudes toward extramarital sexual relations," *Journal of Marriage and the Family* 47 (February 1985): 173–178; and R. T. Coward and W. M. Smith, Jr., "Families in rural society" in D. A. Dillman and D. J. Hobbs, eds., *Rural Society in the U.S.: Issues for the 1980s* (Boulder, Colo.: Westview Press, 1982).

2. Susan Sprecher, Kathleen McKinney, Robert Walsh, and Carrie Anderson, "A revision of the Reiss premarital sexual permissiveness scale," *Journal of Marriage and the Family* 50 (August 1988): 821–828.

3. Manisha Harisingh Maskay and Anne McCreary Juhasz, "The decision-making process model: Design and use for adolescent sexual decisions," *Family Relations* 32 (January 1983): 111; also see S. H. Miller, "A progress report on a study of childbearing and childrearing among 12–15-year-olds" (New York: Research Center Child

Welfare League of America, 1981); Sprecher and others, "A revision," pp. 821–827; and Henry A. Bowman, *Marriage for Moderns* 7th ed. (New York: McGraw–Hill, 1948), pp. 39–43.

4. Paul Gebhard, "Accent on the News," *Milwaukee Journal,* February 20, 1977, p. 1; same general views repeated in press interviews, June 1989.

5. John D. Williams and Arthur P. Jacoby, "The effects of premarital heterosexual and homosexual experience on dating and marriage desirability," *Journal of Marriage and the Family* 51 (May 1989): 492. Between 1982 and 1987 U. of North Dakota females' coital experience increased from 39% to 52%. Findings of four other studies in the 1980s are also cited.

6. Sprecher and others, "A revision," p. 835; Also Ira L. Reiss, *The Social Context of Premarital Sexual Permissiveness* (New York: Holt, Rinehart and Winston, 1967).

7. Sprecher and others, "A revision," pp. 821–828.

8. Statistics taken from the news release by the Tomah (Wisconsin) Senior High School to the *Tomah Journal and Monitor Herald.*

9. Boulder *Daily Camera,* "Church not serving needs of young, study says," March 24, 1990. Report on a research project of the Search Institute, Minneapolis, entitled "Faith, Loyalty, and Congregational Life."

10. Richard F. Hettlinger, *Living with Sex: The Student's Dilemma* (New York: Seabury Press, 1966), chapter 10.

11. Robert R. Bell and Michael Gordon, *The Social Dimensions of Human Sexuality* (Boston: Little, Brown, and Co., 1972), pp. 51–53. See also Kinsey and others, *Sexual Behavior in the Human Male,* p. 364.

12. Leo Carroll, "Concern with AIDS and the sexual behavior of college students," *Journal of Marriage and the Family* 50 (May 1988): 405–411; see also Katie Leishman, "Heterosexuals and AIDS," *Atlantic Monthly* (February 1987): 39–58; and Martha Smilgis, "The big chill: Fear of AIDS," *Time* (February 16, 1987): 50–53.

13. Williams and Jacoby, "The effects," pp. 489–497; see also Jacoby and Williams, "Effects of premarital sexual standards and behavior on dating and marriage desirability," *Journal of Marriage and the Family* 47 (1985): 1,059–1,065; and Joseph Istvan and William Griffitt, "Effects of sexual experience on dating desirability and marriage desirability," *Journal of Marriage and the Family* 42 (1980): 377–385.

14. Ernest Burgess and Paul Wallin, *Engagement and Marriage* (Philadelphia: J. B. Lippincott Co., 1953).

15. Ibid.

16. Kinsey and others, *Sexual Behavior in the Human Female,* pp. 427–428.
17. Shere Hite, *The Hite Report: A Nationwide Study of Female Sexuality* (New York: Dell Publishing Co., Inc., 1976), p. 229: "Only approximately 30% of the women in this study could orgasm regularly from intercourse."
18. Radio interview, WBBM Chicago, October 25, 1977.
19. Arthur A. Rouner, Jr., *Struggling with Sex: A Serious Call to Marriage-centered Sexual Life* (Minneapolis: Augsburg Fortress, 1987).
20. Bill Sands, *My Shadow Ran Fast* (Englewood Park, N.J.: Prentice–Hall, 1969).
21. Hite, *Hite Report,* pp. 248ff.
22. Elaine C. Pierson, *Sex Is Never an Emergency: A Candid Guide for Young Adults,* 3rd ed. (Philadelphia: J. B. Lippincott Co., 1973); see also L. G. Baker, "In my opinion," pp. 297–298.
23. L. G. Baker, "In my opinion," pp. 297–298.
24. Sara Mayer, "Public still doesn't understand the facts of acquaintance rape," *The Boulder* (Colo.) *Sunday Camera* (July 16, 1989): 15A. Ms. Mayer, LCSW, is a therapist and consultant for the Boulder Rape Crisis Team.

## Chapter 11

1. See also Bryan Green, "A basis for sex morality," Part 6, a filmstrip (Malibu, Calif.: Stephen Bosustow Productions).
2. H. W. Long, *Sane Sex Life and Sane Sex Living* (New York: Oak Press, 1961).

## Chapter 12

1. Elise F. Jones and Jacqueline Darroch Forrest, "Contraceptive failure in the United States: Revised estimates from the 1982 National Survey of Family Growth," *Family Planning Perspectives* 21 (May/June 1989): 103–109; also S. K. Henshaw and J. Silverman, "The characteristics and prior contraceptive use of U.S. abortion patients," *Family Planning Perspectives* 20 (1988): 158.
2. Kieran Sawyer, *Sex and the Teenager: Choices and Decisions. Program Director's Manual* (Notre Dame, Ind.: Ave Maria Press, 1990), pp. 59–60. See also Catholic Diocese of Cleveland: Department of Marriage and Family Ministry, "Covenant: Natural Family Planning," (Cleveland, June 1988), p. 7.
3. From Table 5 in E. F. Jones and J. D. Forrest, "Contraceptive failure," p. 109.

4. Matthew 5:28.
5. *Sexuality and Communications*, Association Films, 333 Adelaide St. West, Toronto, Ontario, Canada M5V 1R6.

**Chapter 13**

1. Elsie King, "Personality Characteristics . . . Ideal and Perceived in Relation to Mate Selection," unpublished Ph.D. dissertation, Libraries of the University of Southern California, 1961.
2. Walter Stephan, Ellen Berscheid, and Elaine Walster, "Sexual arousal and heterosexual perception," *Journal of Personality and Social Psychology* 20 (October 1971): 93–101.
3. Sidney M. Jourard and Ardis Whitman, "The fear that cheats us of love," *Redbook* 137 (October 1971): 82–83.
4. Robert O. Blood, Jr., *Marriage*, 2nd ed. (New York: The Free Press, 1969), p. 112.

**Chapter 14**

1. Landis and Landis, *Building Marriage*, p. 117.
2. Kelly, *Courtship*, p. 217.
3. Richard Driscoll, Keith E. Davis, and Milton E. Lipetz, "Parental interference and romantic love: The Romeo and Juliet effect," *Journal of Personality and Social Psychology* 24 (October 1972): 1–10.
4. Harvey J. Locke, *Predicting Adjustment in Marriage: A Comparison of a Divorced and a Happily Married Group* (New York: Henry Holt and Co., Inc., 1951), pp. 75-76; also see Margaret Guminski Cleek and T. Allan Pearson, "Perceived causes of divorce: An analysis of interrelationships," *Journal of Marriage and the Family* 47 (February 1985): 179–183.

**Chapter 15**

1. Carol Kelly, Ted L. Huston, and Rodney M. Cate, "Premarital relationship correlates of the erosion of satisfaction in marriage," *Journal of Social and Personal Relationships* 2 (June 1985): 167–178.

**Chapter 16**

1. George R. Bach and Ronald M. Deutsch, "Conflict: The key to sustained reality" in Carl E. Williams and John F. Crosby, *Choice and Challenge: Contemporary Readings in Marriage* (Dubuque, Iowa: William C. Brown Co., 1974), p. 182.

2. Murray A. Strauss, "Leveling, civility, and violence in the family," *Journal of Marriage and Family* 36 (February 1974).

## Chapter 17

1. Reik, *Of Love,* p. 73.
2. Hirning and Hirning, *Marriage Adjustment,* p. 121; Reik, *Of Love,* p. 71.

## Chapter 18

1. Reik, *Of Love,* p. 20.
2. Hirning and Hirning, *Marriage Adjustment,* p. 282.
3. Luke 17:33.

## Chapter 19

1. Reik, *Of Love,* pp. 101–102.
2. Blood, *Marriage,* p. 108.

## Chapter 20

1. George P. Murdock, *Social Structure* (New York: Free Press, 1965), p. 294. Also William N. Stephens, *Cross-Cultural Perspectives* (New York: Holt, Rinehart and Winston, 1982); and Arlene S. Skolnick, *The Intimate Environment: Exploring Marriage and the Family,* 4th ed. (Boston: Little, Brown, 1987).
2. Skolnick, *Intimate Environment.*
3. McCary, *Freedom and Growth,* p. 48.
4. Booth and Edwards, "Age at marriage," p. 72.
5. Philip Nobile, "Uncommon Conversations: A vote for the 'new fidelity,'" from *Insight Magazine,* in the *Milwaukee Journal,* 13 November 1977, pp. 28, 31.
6. Margaret Mead in Aron M. Krich, ed., *The Anatomy of Love* (New York: Dell Publishing Co., 1960).
7. Skolnick, *Intimate Environment.*
8. Locke, *Predicting Adjustment,* p. 153.
9. Blood, *Marriage,* p. 107.

## Appendix

1. "Many teens misinformed on AIDS," *Family Planning Perspectives* 21 (January/February 1989): 4; also "More are better informed on

AIDS," "Remember that brochure . . . ?" and "U.S. AIDS toll mounts" 21 (May/June 1989): 100, 102. Also, "One-third of infants born to HIV–Positive mothers face illness or death during their first year of life," *Family Planning Perspectives* 21 (November/December 1989): 281–282.

2. Surgeon General C. Everett Koop and the Centers for Disease Control, U.S. Public Health Service, "Understanding AIDS" (Washington, D.C.: Government Printing Office, 1988).

3. "Teens and AIDS: Opportunities for prevention," Adolescent Pregnancy Prevention Clearinghouse, *Children's Defense Fund* (Washington, D.C., November 1988).